Knox's Colleague

Knox's Colleague: The Life & Catechisms of John Craig

Kyle McDanell, ed.

ISBN: 1493782975
ISBN-13: 978-1493782970

To my wife, whom I love more than words can express.
-Song of Solomon 8:6-7

CONTENTS

PREFACE

Christianity has traditionally been a confessional faith dependant on deep historic doctrines. The gospel, revealed in the pages of Scripture, is the historic story of God's intervention into a fallen world for the sake of His glory and for the redemption of man. Thus from its conception, Christians have expressed this theological story through means of confessions, catechisms, and creeds. Some of the earliest creeds even found their way into the New Testament in what some believe to be christological hymns with Philippians 2:6-11 and 1 Corinthians 15:3-4 being the most notable. The apostles encouraged the church to affirm and "contend earnestly for the faith which was once for all handed down to the saints" (Jude 3). The gospel, to the first Christians, was a transcendent message that united all nations, languages, cultures, backgrounds, and socioeconomics. Thus the faith, and the doctrines it stood upon, had to be preserved.

The generations following the apostles continued this doctrine-affirming trend by limiting orthodoxy to a set of theological truths in what some referred to as the Rule of Faith. Anything contradictory to the Rule of Faith was deemed heretical. In his book *The Prescription Against the Heretics*, Tertullian (160-225) argued that orthodoxy was limited to a set of immutable beliefs including theology proper, cosmology, christology, pneumetology, the atonement, the resurrection and ascension of Jesus, and eschatology. He wrote:

> Now, with regard to this rule of faith – that we may from this point acknowledge what it is which we defend – it is, you must know, that which prescribes the belief that there is only one God, and that He is none other than the Creator of the world, who produced all things out of nothing through His own Word, first of all sent forth; that this Word is called His Son, *and*, under the name of God, was seen "in diverse manners" by the patriarchs, heard at all times in the prophets, at last brought down by the Spirit and Power of the Father into the Virgin Mary, was made flesh in her womb, and, being born of her, went forth as Jesus Christ; thenceforth He preached the new law and the new promise of the kingdom of heaven, worked miracles; having been crucified, He rose again the third day; then having ascended into the heavens, He sat at the right hand of the Father; sent instead of Himself the Power of the Holy Ghost to lead such as

> believe; will come with glory to take the saints to the enjoyment of everlasting life and of the heavenly promises, and to condemn the wicked to everlasting fire, after the resurrection of both these classes shall have happened, together with the restoration of their flesh. This rule . . . was taught by Christ, and raises amongst ourselves no other questions than those which heresies introduce, and which make men heretics.[1]

This "rule of faith," was standard among the early Christians. In a similar fashion, another early church father, Irenaeus (130-202), argued for what he called the "Canon of Truth." One example comes in the first book of *Against Heresies*. He writes:

> The Church, though dispersed through out the whole world, even to the ends of the earth, has received from the apostles and their disciples this faith: [She believes] in one God, the Father Almighty, maker of heaven, and earth, and the sea, and all things that are in them; and in one Christ Jesus, the Son of God, who became incarnate for our salvation; and in the Holy Spirit, who proclaimed throught the prophets the dispensations of God, and the advents, and the birth from a virgin, and the passion, and the resurrection from the dead, and the ascension into heaven in the flesh of the beloved Christ Jesus, our Lord, and His future manifestation from heaven in the glory of the Father "to gather all things in one," and to raise up anew all flesh of the whole human race, in order that to Christ Jesus, our Lord, and God, and

---

[1] Tertullian, *The Prescription Against the Heretics*, 3:29.

> Savior, and King, according to the will of the invisible Father, "every knee should bow, of things in heaven, and things in earth, and things under the earth, and that every tongue should confess to Him, and that he should execute just judgment toward all; that He may send "spiritual wickedness," and the angels who transgressed and became apostates, together with the ungodly, and unrighteous, and wicked, and profane among men, into everlasting fire; but may, in the exercise of His grace, confer immortality on the righteous, and holy, and those who have kept His commandments, and have persevered in His love, some from the beginning of their Christian course, and others from the date of their repentance, and may surround them with everlasting glory.[2]

The first centuries of the church would eventually declare this faith by means of creeds which defined more universally Christian orthodoxy. The first of these creeds is the Apostle's Creed which remains influential today. The second was written in the fourth century in response to the Arian heresy which denied the deity of Jesus Christ. This creed, known as the Nicene Creed, was adopted in 325 and articulates orthodox Christology. Later a more developed christological creed was written and adopted by the church known as the Chalcedonian Creed (451).

These three ecumenical creeds are the most notable creeds of the first half millennia of the church and remain

---

[2] Irenaeus, *Againist Heresies*, 1.10.1.

influential definitions of theological truths today. It should come to no surprise that orthodox believers, even today, continue to affirm and recite these relevant creeds which articulate and defend transcendent and immutable doctrines of the faith across all cultures, languages, and time.

Yet as the church marched through the Middle Ages, the Roman Catholic Church and its pontiff increased in power and new doctrines were added to the faith. Catholic doctrine placed tradition and the papacy on par with Scripture as authoritative. This led the Catholic Church to adopt several doctrines later rejected by the Protestant Reformers. These include the Pope as the head of the Church, transubstantiation, a refusal to give laity the bread, prayer to the saints, a duet of faith and works for salvation, an all-Latin mass, and the selling of indulgence with the promise of personal salvation. This last Catholic doctrine led one 16th century monk-turn-pastor-and-doctor-of-theology to revolt. When Martin Luther (1483-1546) nailed his *95 Theses* to the Wittenburgh Castle church door in 1517, the theological world was rocked and the Protestant Reformation had officially begun.[3]

---

[3] This is not to suggest that Luther was the first to call out the abuses of the church. Two leading pre-Reformers include John

In protesting the Roman Catholic Church, the Reformation recovered the ancient gospel. This radical turn away from Roman Catholic doctrine required new creeds and confession of faiths. Thus the 16th Century saw a swell of confessions. These include Martin Luther's Large and Small Catechisms (1529), The Augsburg Confession (1530), The First (1536) and Second (1562) Helvetic Confessions, The Lausanne Articles (1536), The Geneva Confession (1536), The French Confession of Faith (1559), The Scottish Confession of Faith (1560), The Belgic Confession of Faith (1561), The Heidelberg Catechism (1563), and many others.[4] Though each Protestant movement affirmed the ecumenical confessions of Nicea and Chalcedon as well as the Apostle's Creed, the Reformers perceived the recovered ancient faith needed to be broadened and more clearly defined. The ancient creeds

---

Wycliffe (1330-1384) and John Huss (1369-1415). Luther would later be compared to Huss who was burned at the stake for challenging the Roman Catholic Church. Luther considered that comparison to be a badge of honor. Many of the portraits and paintings of Luther include a goose, representing Huss, over his shoulder. Luther certainly was not the first to call for reformation.

[4] For a collection of Reformed catechisms and creeds see James T. Dennison, *Reformed Confessiosn of the 16th and 17th Centuries in English Translation*, 4 volumes (Grand Rapids, MI: Reformation Heritage, 2008-2014).

were written in response to trinitarian and christological heresies (like Arianism in the 4th century). Since the Reformers were responding to Roman Catholic doctrine, it was necessary to compose confessions that clearly defined their separation from Rome.

The Reformation in Scotland was no different. John Knox (1514-1572) was its leading figure who returned to Scotland, from a type of exile, in 1559 after spending a number of years in Geneva with John Calvin. Upon his return, he immediately moved Scotland to adopt Reformed (Calvinist) doctrine. The first major creed in Knox's Scotland was the *Scottish Confession of Faith* adopted in 1560.

Decades later, the Scottish Kirk commissioned former Dominican friar and colleague of Knox, John Craig (1512-1600), to compose two catechisms for the church which are found in this book. The first catechism, ironcially titled *A Short Summary of the Whole Catechism Wherein the Question is Proposed and Answered in Few Words For the Greater Ease of the Common People and Children*, published in 1581 in Scotland and 1589 in England, is the longest of the two and became a "Scots staple."[5] History has titled it more simply as

---

[5] Dennison, *Reformed Confessinos of the 16th and 17th Centuries in English Translation*, vol. 3, 544.

Craig's Catechism. Attached to the catechism was the *Negative Confession* (also known as *The King's Confession*), written by Craig, which was a covenant between the king and the people of Scotland assuring that Scotland would remain Protestant free from any influence of Rome. This confession eventually became the first part of the *National Covenant* of 1628. *Craig's Catechism*, "was the first Scottish Catechism to come into widespread use in the Kirk."[6]

Eleven years after *Craig's Catechism* was published, the Scottish Kirk commissioned him to pen a shorter catechism for the examination of young people partaking in their first communion. Its was first published in 1592 as *A Form of Examination Before the Communion Approved by the General Assembly of the Kirk of Scotland And Appointed to be Used in Families and Schools with the Short Latin Catechism Commonly Taught in Schools*, but history has titled it more simply as *Communion Catechism.* It was based primarily on the earlier *Craig's Catechism* following the brief question and answer format covering the basic tenents of the faith.

Both catechisms were in common use until they were supersceded by the larger and shorter Westminister Catechisms (1647). As a result, "The evangelical and

---

[6] Thomas F. Torrance, *The School of Faith: The Catechisms of the Reformed Church* (Eugene, OR: Wipf & Stock Publishers), 97.

theological heart of this old Scottish tradition was taught in the catechisms of John Craig" and others.[7]

It could be argued, rather boldly perhaps, that as Martin Luther had his Philip Melanchthon, Ulrich Zwingli had his Heinrich Bullinger, and John Calvin had his Theodore Beze, so too John Knox had his John Craig. But of these colleagues, Craig has almost been forgotten even though he played an influential role in the Scottish Reformation and in the development of its theology.

That is why this volume has been published. Both the story of Knox's colleague and his catechisms must be shared again for a new generation. Craig's work in Scotland is a work of God's providence that saved him from the eve of his own execution. This former Domincan Friar dedicated the rest of his spared life to promote the cause of Reformed theology among his own countrymen. He preached, wrote, ministered, and served the Scottish Kirk for decades. When Knox was unavailable, usually due to expulsion, Craig would often serve as his replacement. Knox famously made Mary Queen of Scots cry. Carrying on that same tradition, Craig would later cause her

---

[7] Thomas F. Torrance, *Scottish Theology: From John Knox to John McLeod Campbell* (Edinburgh: T & T Clark, 1996), 50.

successor, King James VI of Scotland, to cry.[8]

In the pages that follow, Craig's story is more fully chronicled from the pen of historian Thomas Graves Law (1836-1904) who has written the best available biography of Craig. Law highlights Craig's remarkable story and the influence of his writings apart from myths commonly attached to him.

In addition to Law's biography, this volume includes a modernized reading of Craig's two catechisms.[9] For the sake of history and to promote the influence of John Craig and his catechisms on the Scottish Reformation and the reformed faith, this book has been published. Both catechisms have been updated and modernized by the editor while only minor corrections and changes have been made to Bonar's biography. The goal is for history to be preserved, sound Reformed theology promoted, and the words and works of one of Scotland's great theological and pastoral leaders celebrated.

---

[8] King James VI of Scotland is better known for the Bible translation named after him: the King James Bible originally published in 1611 – eleven years after Craig's death.

[9] Another modern reading of Craig's two catechisms can be found in Torrance, *The School of Faith* and Dennison, *Reformed Confessinos of the 16th and 17th Centuries in English Translation*, vol. 3.

Why John Craig Matters

Before moving on, perhaps it is best to highlight why this rather obscure and unfamiliar Scottish Reformer is worth our attention. First, Craig reminds us that history is complete with individuals who were used mightily by God but have been forgotten by history and historians. If it were not for the age of the Internet and the curiosity of persons like me, Craig's work and influence might have been lost. But from the perspective of the throne of God, such saints benefit from their reward of faithful service. Fortunately, modern technology allows for historians and theologians to preserve the names and works of lesser known believers for future generations.

Similarly, Craig reminds us of the importance of other, lesser known Reformers of the 16th century. Martin Luther, for example, considered his colleague, Philip Melanchthon, one of the greatest theologians of his time.[10] The Great Reformers, like Calvin, Luther, Knox, and Zwingli were not isolated theological giants, but were

---

[10] In his *Bondage of the Will*, Luther praised Melanchthon's *Loci* as an "unsurpassed volume on the doctrines of theology." He then adds "That book of his, to my mind, deserves not merely to live as long as books are read, but to take its place in the Church's canon." Martin Luther, *The Bondage of the Will*, translated and edited by J. I. Packer and O. R. Johnston (Grand Rapids, MI: Revel, 1957), 62, 63.

leaders of great thinkers raised up by God for such a time of theological reform. A study of Craig reminds us that limiting the Reformation to a handful of leaders prevents a fuller picture of God's providential work of grace during this period.

Thirdly, Craig's theology remains relevant. Orthodoxy, itself, is relevant because the gospel is transcendent. Craig articulates a reformed presbyterian theology common at his time and in ours. His catechisms artfully articulate the faith once for all delivered to the saints (Jude 3). That is the nature of theology. The gospel is never in need of an update. The same faith that rocked the world in the first and the sixteenth centuries remains powerful and adequate enough for our day as well.

This is the real weakness of modern and postmodern liberalism. From the beginning, liberal theology sought to rescue Christianity from itself. Liberal theologians, from Friedrich Schleiermacher to John Shelby Spong, have assumed orthodox doctrines were outdated and no longer relevant for a post-Englightenment age. This liberal experiment, however, has proven to be a farce. In their persuit of relevancy they have made their articulation of the faith irrelevant. Liberalism does not save. In this sense, Craig's almost-forgotten catechisms of over four hundred years ago are more relevant than the latest liberal attempt to redefine the gospel and save the faith.

Finally, the resurgence of Reformed theology, often referred to as the New Calvinism or Young, Restless, and Reformed Movement,[11] has led to an increased interests in Reformed theologians of the past. This rise of Reformed theology can be traced to several factors, but no doubt the undying influence of Calvinist theological giants like Charles Spurgeon and Martin Llyod-Jones along with the tireless work of Banner of Truth Publishers and others who have republished Puritan and other Reformed theology works for many decades have played a major role in this theological resurgence. While the rest of the world becomes more progressive and secular, the church appears to be turning more toward traditional doctrines of God's sovereignty, divine election, and total depravity. This has led to an increase interests in the Reformation itself. Martin Luther and the other reformers remain as popular as ever. With the rising tide of secularism, the old, old story is becoming more, more relevant and timely.

In regards to his theology, Craig has much to offer

---

[11] Both nicknames found their way in the title of the book by Collin Hanson, *Young, Restless, and Reformed: A Journalist's Journey with the New Calvinists* (Wheaton, IL: Crossway, 2008).

especially to those new to Reformed doctrine. His treatment of divine election, for example, serves as an excellent summary and introduction. In his longer catechism, Craig asks a series of short questions regarding the genesis of our justification, sanctification, and glorification. Well in line with Reformed thought, such doctrinal truths are found, he argues, in the sovereign will and grace of God. "Out of what fountain," Craig asks, "does our stability flow?" Simply, "Out of God's eternal and unchanging election in Christ."

This one answer adequately summarizes the great doctrines of Reformed theology. Because God elects us, ("By his effectual calling in due time,") the believer is justified by Christ, perpectually and inseparably unified "with Christ," continually being sanctified,[12] obedient to God's Word, victorious "against Satan and sin," all with "A sure seal of our election and glorification."

Furthermore, Craig's catechisms, especially his communion catechism, are "perhaps the most Christological of them all."[13] T. F. Torrance highlights three features of Craig's work that, he says, "deserves

---

[12] Craig writes, "Q. What works sanctification? A. The hatred of sin and love of godliness."

[13] Torrance, *The School of Faith*, xv.

notice." First, "It is more concerned than" most of the other catechisms of its time "with the understanding of the Gospel in the light of the whole history of Redemption." Secondly, "Its concern both for the doctrine of the person and work of Christ and for personal faith lays great emphasis upon union and communion with Christ in the Communion of the Saints." Finally, Torrance highlights "The combination of the evangelical and sacramental 'moments' in the teaching and the life of the Church."[14]

A full treatment of Torrance's argument goes beyond the purpose of this preface, but perhaps his first point is worth noting. Along with the rise of the New Calvinism has come a welcomed emphasis among young pastors, writers, and theologians to emphasize the gospel. This is seen in a plethora of books on the gospel along with countless resources showing how to read the Bible, especially the Old Testament, Christologically. Long before young seminarians were discovering the "Christ throughout the Scriptures" hermeneutic, Craig influenced generations of believers with the same approach. Craig was well ahead of his time.

In all of this, Craig must not be forgotten. His story only bears testimony to the doctrine of providence he

[14] Ibid., xix-xx.

articulates in this volume. His theology remains as true today as it was over four centuries ago.[15] Knox, Craig, and others in the Scottish Kirk stood boldly against Kings, Queens, Popes, and the Roman Church in defense of the gospel and God used them providencially as His instruments of grace to preserve the faith. It is very possible, almost five hundred years later, that God is about to do it again.

Thus Craig remains an important voice even though he is at risk of being forgotten by scholars, theologians, and even history itself. I believe that the story of the Scottish Reformation remains incomplete without a serious consideration of the influence and work of John Craig. This volume is a small effort in restoring the honor he deserves.

---

[15] As a confessional Baptist I have honest disagreements with Craig and other reformed Scottish theologians of the 16th Century. That is not my point in this present work. I am arguing that the recovery of the gospel and the defense of God's revelation is preserved in Craig's work and that message remains prescient today.

JOHN CRAIG (1512-1600)

By

Thomas Graves Law

The following is a biography of John Craig from the pen of historian Thomas Graves Law (1836–1904). It originally appeared as the introduction in his reprint of Craig's long catechism called *A Shorte Summe of the Whole Catechism* (published in 1883) and later included in the book *Collected Essays and Review of Thomas Graves Law* edited by P. Hume Brown in 1904. It remains the best available biography of the Scottish Reformer. Law tells Craig's story free from the numerous legends common in other biographies. Throughout the narrative, Law interacts with other historians and sources in order to uncover the real John Craig. In the end, Law shows that though the myths are fascinating, the real story surpasses all embellishments.

This edition of Law's biography of Craig has been modernized along with minor editorial changes for the purpose of readability. The editor has sought to preserve the original intent of its author.

The first edition of *A Shorte Summary of the Whole Catechism* by John Craig, printed at Edinburgh by Henrie Charteris in 1581, a work of great authority in its day, is one of the rarest of early printed Scottish books. Neither the British Museum, the Bodleian, nor any of the Scottish Universities can boast of its possession. The late Mr. David Laing made diligent search for it for many years, but without success. The editor knows of but two copies, one in the Advocates' Library and the other among the rare bibliographical treasures of his kind and valued friend, Mr. James Gibson Craig. It is at his request and in accordance with his instructions that the present facsimile reprint has been prepared from the copy in his possession. The Catechism has been indeed frequently reprinted, but all the early editions are extremely scarce, and have been almost lost sight of by bibliographers. It was printed in London by John Wolfe in 1583, and again by Robert Waldegrave in 1584, by Thomas Orwin in 1589, and by Robert Harrison in 1597. In Edinburgh an edition was printed by John

Wreittoun in 1632.[16] Dr. Horatius Bonar has recently reproduced that of 1597 in his collection of *Catechisms of the Scottish Reformation*, London, 1866.

At the end of his *Catechism,* Craig printed the *Confession of Faith*, or *National Covenant*, which he had drawn up a few months before at the desire of James VI, and which was subscribed by the king and his household, January 28, 1580-1. The origin of this famous document, with signatures attached, is preserved in the Advocates Library. In publishing it as an Appendix to his *Catechism*, the author "thought good to add, for the better confirmation of this confession, the judgment of the ancient and godly Fathers concerning the authority of the holy scriptures," and next, "the open and shameless blasphemies of the late Papists, spued out and written in contempt" of the same.

This larger Catechism should not be confounded, as it has been by several writers, with an abridged work of a similar character, first published by Craig in 1591-2, entitled, *A Form of Examinatiion Before the Communion.*[17] This

---

[16] Lowndes mentions only the first edition and a reprint at London in 1591; but there is some doubt if any reprint was made at that date.

[17] The Catechism of 1581 was unknown to Mr. James Scott, the author of the *Lives of the Protestant Reformrs in Scotland*, who communicated in 1811 several articles, signed I.S.P., to the "Edinburgh Christian Instruction on the Life of John Craig." It

smaller Catechism was prepared by the direction of the General Assembly, August 1590. In July 1591, the Assembly "thought it meant to be imprinted, being be the author thereof contradict in some shorter bounds," and in May 1592[18] it was decreed "that every pastor travel with his flock that they may buy the same book and read it in their families whereby they may be better instructed and that the same be read and learned in Lector's Schools in place of the little Catechism," i.e. of "The Manner to Examine Children," at the end of Calvin's Catechism. This "Form of Examination" frequently reprinted, will be found described as "Craig's Catechism" in Dunlops *Collection of Confessions of Faith*, etc., Edinb, 1722. It has also been included in the *Collection* of Dr. Horatius Bonar.

It may be well to mention here some other works attributed to this divine. In 1565 Craig, in conjunction with John Knox, composed the treatise on fasting, entitled, "The Order and Doctrine of the General Fast, Appointed by the General Assembly of the Church of Scotland: Halden at Edinburgh the 25 Day of December, 1565. Set

---

was unknown also to Tytler (*Life of Sir Thomas Craig*, p. 26) and to Dr. Hew Scott (*Fafti Eccles.* Scot. Pt. i. p. 150), nor is any reference made to it in the Encycl. Britanica (ninth edition, art. *Catechism* and *Craig*).

18 *Book of the Universal Kirk*, 774, 784, 788.

down by John Knox and John Craig at the Appointment of the Assembly." This is also reprinted in Dunlop's *Collection*. Again, in August 1590, it was ordained by the General Assembly that "the brethren of the presbytery of Edinburgh should peruse an answer set out by Mr. Craig against a pernicious writing put out against the Confession of Faith, together with the Preface made by Mr. P. Davidson."[19] But it does not appear that this work was ever committed to print. There is little doubt, however, that Craig was the translator of fifteen Psalms, which bear the signature "I. C.," in the Metrical Psalter, printed at Edinburgh in 1565.[20]

Notwithstanding the very important part which Craig played in the foundation of the Protestant Kirk, and the influence which he wielded in all the affairs of his country luring the space of forty years, he has left behind him but scanty materials for a biography. We possess neither his sermons nor his correspondence, not even his portrait. It is mainly from the minutes of the General Assemblies, where his legal knowledge and habits of business were in great request, that we gather the amount of silent work done by him in favor of the cause which he had espoused.

---

[19] M'Crie, *Life of Melville*, p. 224; *Book of Universal Kirk*, p. 777.
[20] Livingston's *Scottish Metrical Psalter*, p. 27.

Archbishop Spottiswoode has put on record a fair estimate of the character of this strenuous opponent of prelacy: "This man whiled he lived was held in good esteem, a great divine and excellent preacher, of a grave behavior, sincere, inclining to no faction, and, which increased his reputation, living honestly, without ostentation or desire of outward glory."[21]

The antecedents of the men who became the principal agents in the ecclesiastical revolutions of the sixteenth century are always of much interest. The early life of John Craig was remarkable for its vicissitudes and adventures, and the training which he went through is not without significance in its bearing on his subsequent career. He was born in 1512, and belonged to the same family as the illustrious lawyer Sir Thomas Craig of Riccarton, who, it appears, was his near relation and at one time his pupil. His father was slain at the field of Flodden. John completed his education at the university of St. Andrews, and then passed into England where he became tutor to the children of Lord Dacres. After two years he returned to Scotland and joined the Dominicans in their house at St. Andrews. He there fell under suspicion of heresy — on what point we are not informed — but apparently he

---

[21] Spottiswoode, ed. 1851, vol. iii. p. 91.

cleared himself without difficulty, and after a short imprisonment went back to England about the year 1536, with the hope of getting to Cambridge through the influence of his friend Lord Dacres. Failing in this he went abroad and made his way to Rome, where he attracted the notice of Cardinal Pole. The Cardinal, who held moderate opinions upon many points of controversy between the churches and may have had some influence in forming the mind of young Craig, then about twenty-four years of age, procured for him admission into a convent of the Dominicans at Bologna. Here Craig appears to have won esteem and distinction. It may be presumed that he became a priest, but it is not clear whether he was ordained in Scotland or in Italy. At Bologna he was made Master of Novices, an office which implies in its bearer a reputation for piety, as well as an influence over men. His practical talents, moreover, led to his employment in various commissions on certain affairs of his Order in Italy and in the Island of Chios; and on his return he was made Rector of the Dominican College.

Craig at this time must have been well grounded in the theological science of the Church to which he belonged. Bologna was a flourishing centre of Catholic learning. Craig must have been there in 1547, when the Council of

Trent was transferred to that city, where its second session was held in the palace of the archbishop. The doctrines of the German Reformers had however penetrated even into the strongholds of the Pontifical territory. John Mollio had in his lectures at the university used dangerous language on points of theology which brought upon him a citation to Rome, an admonition to abstain in future from expositions of St. Paul, and finally, at the request of the archbishop, his removal from the university. Martin Bucer, in 1541, congratulates the Protestants of the city on their progress, and a few years later they can boast of being able to raise, if need be, 6,000 soldiers to fight against the Pope.[22] Yet there is nothing to show that Craig entertained any strong inclinations towards the new learning or had in any way lost the confidence of his superiors until many years later. One day, in the library of the Inquisition, he fell in with a copy of *Calvin's Institutes*, with which he was much impressed. He appears to have confided his now altered state of mind to a venerable friar, a Scotsman by birth according to one tradition,[23] who, while expressing his entire sympathy with his friend, earnestly warned him to keep his own counsel, or to seek refuge in some Protestant

---

[22] M'Crie's *Reformation in Italy*, ed. 1827, 79, 83.
[23] M'Crie's *Life of Knox*, ed. 1839, p. 238.

country, Craig, however, made no secret of his new opinions, and consequently soon found himself once more a prisoner, and this time within the walls of the Inquisition at Rome. Here he was confined for nine months, thrown, if we may trust the narrative of John Row, into "a base prison, or rather pit, which the Tibris River flowed, so that the prisoners stood in water sometimes almost to their middle."

With Paul IV, who then occupied the papal chair, Craig seemed to have but small chance of escape. The chief interests of this rigorous and austere pontiff centered in the Inquisition, which he had been the means of restoring. He was busy during his pontificate with enlarging its jurisdiction and in legislating for its action, and in his zeal against heretics he authorized the application of torture for the detection of their accomplices. In his dying moments he commended his favorite institution to the care of the cardinals. He expired on the 18th of August 1559. On the 19th Craig was to be burned. The Pope had not been popular. As soon as his death was made known there were riots in the city, the mob broke in pieces the statue which had been erected to him, set fire to the buildings of the Inquisition, ill-used its officers, and let all the prisoners go free.

Craig, after his hairbreadth escape from martyrdom seems to have sought refuge for a time in the suburbs of Rome. Meanwhile a company, either of bandits or papal soldiers sent to arrest the runaway, came upon his hiding place and his life or his liberty was once more in danger. But the good fortune which had opened for him so unexpectedly the doors of his prison did not desert him. The leader of the band took Craig aside and asked him if he did not remember a poor wounded soldier in Bologna who, in dire distress, had begged of him some relief. Craig answered that he did not. "But I do," said the other, "and I am the man." It turned out that Craig had shown great kindness to the soldier, who now, to repay the debt, at some personal risk helped Craig with money and counsel to make good his escape. Spottiswoode says that Craig returned to Bologna, where he trusted some former acquaintances would befriend him, but finding that they "looked strange," and fearing to be again entrapped, he slipped away to Milan and then to Vienna.

The only original sources for this portion of Craig's life are the "Histories of Spottiswoode and Row,"[24] who

[24] Spottiswoode, vol. iii., 91-93; Row's *History of the Kirk of Scotland* (Wodrow Society), Coronis, p. 415, and *Additions to the Coronois*, 457-461.

differ in many points of detail. Row tells the story of the adventure with the soldiers twice over and with considerable fullness but with some discrepancies between the two accounts. He says nothing of a second visit to Bologna and gives a more Protestant complexion to the conduct of Craig throughout. He moreover supposes that between the period of Craig's conversion and his delation for heresy, there was an interval during which he had charge of the education of some children in the family of an Italian nobleman who professed the Reformed faith. This nobleman and other companions of Craig, it is said, shared the latter's imprisonment and escape, but were carried back to the Inquisition by the soldier who had connived at the flight of the friar. Dr. M'Crie, in his *Life of Knox*, adopting this version of the story, states that Craig "obtained his discharge" from the Dominican convent at Bologna. It would be interesting if from original documents at Bologna or Rome the facts of the case, and the character of his convictions at this time, could be ascertaind with certainty. There can be little doubt that at Vienna he preached as a Dominican friar.

In the meantime another incident occurred on his journey, which, says Spottiswoode,

I should scarce relate, so incredible it seems, if too

> many of good place he himself had not often repeated it as a singular testimony of God's care of him, and this it was. When he had travelled some days, declining the highways out of fear, he came into a forest, a wild and desert place, and being so wearied he laid down among some bushes on the side of a little brook to refresh himself. Lying there pensive and full of thoughts (for neither knew he in where he was nor had he any means to bear him out of the way), a dog came fawning with a purse in his teeth and laid it down before him. He, stricken with fear, rose up and, looking about if any were coming that way, when he saw none, took it and construing the same to proceed from God's favorable providence towards him, followed his way until he came to a little village, where he met with some that were travelling to Vienna, in Austria, and changing his intended course went in their company thither.

Row tells substantially the same story, but with additional circumstances and signs of legendary growth:

> Mr. Craig did boast the dog from him, fearing that he should have been challenged for stealing so pretty a dog, but the dog would not be boasted from him, but followed him a space out of the town. . . . At last Mr. Craig began to make of the dog and was content seeing he would not go back to take him to bear him company in his travels and so the dog followed him for some days and waited carefully on him as his master

And it was not until later on when Craig, overcome with heat and fatigue, took himself to prayer, that:

> His dog, his kind fellow-traveller, came to him and . . .

> Mr. Craig looked up, and saw in the dog's mouth a full purse. The dog shook the purse upon Mr. Craig offering it to him: he was astonished and feared to touch the purse, but the dog looked kindly in his face . . . Mr. Craig took the purse out of the dog's mouth and, opening it, found a purse full of gold – all of one kind of gold . . . and being then well provided, he traveled on and, after some stay in France, he came home to Scotland and brought with him to Edinburgh the dog, the purse, and some of the gold.[25]

"This," adds Row:

> though it may seem fabulous to some, I know it to be certain as any human thing can be for the wife of this worthy servant of Jesus Christ, living in Edinburgh (where he was one of the town ministers and very honest, straight, and famous in his time), surviving her husband for many years, until the year 1630, did often relate this history with all the passages of it to me and many others. She was an honest woman, *fide digna*, well known in Edinburgh under the name of Dame Craig.

It is evident that the episode of the dog obtained some notoriety during Craig's lifetime and the mysterious character of the facts was apparently not denied by his

---

[25] This portion of Row's narrative is accepted as historical by Dr. Scott, *Fafti Eccles.* Scot., vol. i., 82. An account of Craig's foreign adventures will be found also in Dr. M'Crie's *Life of Knox* (sixth ed., 236-240), and more briefly in Tytler's *Life of Sir Thomas Craig*. The story of the dog is quoted by George Sinclair, Professor of Philosphy in the University of Glasgow, in his *Satan's Invisible World Discovered*, where it certainly appears, as Mr. Hill Burton remarks (Hist. of Scotland, vol. v., 149), "in rather awkward company."

bitterest theological opponents. The comments upon it made by Dr. John Hamilton, a secular priest and a very able champion of Catholicism, are worth reproducing if only to illustrate the methods of controversy in use in his day and the value of his information. In his "Facile Treatise: Contend First and Infallible Rule to Discern True From False Religion," etc., published at Lou vain in 1600, Hamilton, after some strong denunciations of the marriages of the Reformers, wrote:

> 'We have one notable example of Friar John Craig, who cast off his cowl, [after embracing the Reformed faith. He survived fleeing to Scotland from Italy] because a black dog gave him a purse of gold. The color of the dog may declare if it was a good spirit or not for the Holy Spirit descended upon Christ in the likeliness of a white dove for this apostasy this defrocked friar was made an apostle of this first Evangel in Edinburgh; . . . married a young [woman] of what is a sacrilegious marriage sprang out a cursed generation as the inhabitants and one of the chief ministers of Edinburgh can bear witness.'[26]

It is scarcely necessary to remark that this last statement, which may be due to the same imagination which supplied the color of the dog, cannot be reconciled with the facts. But to return.

---

[26] Facile Treatise, 439. See the comments of Lord Hailes (*Life of John Hamilton*, 11), who quotes the greater part of this passage.

At Vienna, Craig met with a favorable reception. Spottiswoode says that he preached before Maximilian II, who "liking the man and the manner of his preaching would have detained him," and several writers, in relating the circumstance, have repeated the error of supposing that the fugitive friar was befriended by the Emperor. But Maximilian did not succeed his father Ferdinand in the imperial throne until July 1564, about four years after Craig had left Vienna. As archduke, however, Maximilian had already incurred the displeasure of his more Catholic father, as well as of the pope, for his marked leaning towards Lutheran doctrines and his correspondence with the leaders of the Protestant party. In 1558, Paul IV hesitated to recognise Ferdinand as Emperor, and severely blamed him for being the cause of his son's alienation from the Catholic faith by having given him a heretical education. The reproaches of the pope gave a fresh stimulus to Maximilian's opposition to the Roman church, and at this moment he was, no doubt, more than usually inclined to listen with pleasure to one who had so recently been a sufferer from the same pope's persecuting zeal. Craig was, however, at Vienna only a short time before the turning of the tide. Pius IV, the successor of Paul, showed a more conciliatory disposition towards the imperial family, sent the celebrated Hofius to discuss matters of controversy with Maximilian, and, at the intercession of Ferdinand, went so far as to grant the chalice to the laity at Communion, the refusal of which had been a subject of much scruple with the archduke. Before Maximilian ascended the throne he had become again reconciled to his father's creed. Meanwhile the news of Craig's presence in Vienna had reached the pope's ear and he wrote insisting on the restitution of the condemned heretic to the authorities of the Inquisition. The archduke, fortunately, preferred to send him with letters of safe-conduct through Germany into England, where, learning of the ecclesiastical changes which had just taken place in his native country, Craig hastened to Edinburgh and at once offered his services to the Reformed Church.

Craig made his first appearance as a Protestant minister of the Scottish Church in the little chapel of St. Magdalen, in the Cowgate, where he preached to a select number of learned men in Latin; for it is said that during his absence abroad for twenty-four years, he had to some extent lost the use of his native language. Among his hearers at this time was probably the accomplished young scholar Thomas Craig, before mentioned, who, having also just returned from abroad, where he had studied in the

French universities, now placed himself under the guidance of his relative with a view to completing his higher education before passing advocate which he did in 1563.[27] In 1561 Craig was appointed minister at Holyrood House, an appointment which had been little more than nominal after the arrival of Queen Mary in the month of August. In April of the following year, the town council agreed to invite him to act as the assistant of John Knox at St. Giles. This was at the request of Knox himself, who had been hitherto unassisted, except by his reader John Cairns. In July of 1562 the General Assembly approved of the translation, but it does not appear to have been finally carried out until the following year. In the High Kirk, and under the influence of the great reformer, Craig soon recovered the vigorous use of his mother tongue, and the boldness of his speech in inveighing against the courtiers elicited the approbation of his colleague who quotes from a sermon of that "worthy servant of God" some passages which especially excited the wrath of Secretary William Maitland.

In June 1564 there took place a remarkable conference, which was held between certain deputies from the General Assembly on the one hand and the ministers

---

[27] Tytler's *Life of Sir Thomas Craig*, 22, 29.

of the Crown on the other. The special object of Maitland, the proposer of the conference, was to restrain the license of preachers in dealing with the conduct of the queen, but the general question of the amount of obedience due from subjects to their sovereigns was brought into free discussion.

Knox and Maitland were the principal speakers and the argument was conducted with admirable skill on both sides. Knox forced Maitland to admit that if the queen were to become a persecutor, he would be ready to adopt the doctrine of his opponent; but "the question before us," he insisted, "is, whether we may or may not suppress the queen's mass." "Idolatry," answered Knox, "ought not only to be suppressed, but the idolater ought to die the death."

"I know," replied Maitland, "that the idolater ought to die, but by whom?" "By the people," insisted Knox. Finally, after a lengthy debate, the opinions of all present were challenged in turn. Douglas, the rector of the University of St. Andrews, with whom agreed John Wynram, the superintendent of Fife, took the more moderate side.

"If the queen," said Douglas, "oppose herself to our religion, which is the only true religion, the nobility and states of the realm professing the same may justly oppose themselves to her. As concerning the mass, I know it is idolatry, yet I am not resolved whether that by violence we may take it from her."

Others voted more decidedly, that "as the mass is an abominable idolatry, so ought it to be repressed and that by so doing men did no more wrong to the queen's Majesty than those who should by force take from her a poisoned cup when she was going to drink it."

The question in dispute is one of particular interest, as it presents the single point of contact between the principles of the extreme presbyterian party and those of the extreme partisans of the pope. Cardinal Allen, in maintaining that heretical sovereigns are deprived of their dominions by the law of Christendom *ipfo facto*, did not forget to support the papal pretensions by those Knox. It is instructive to note that the passages from the Old Testament, used by the cardinal to show that in the deposition of lawfully created kings God made use of the ministry of priests and prophets, are just those which were brought forward by the Reformer in this famous conference.[28]

Craig does not seem to have expressed any opinion at

---

[28] *Sincere and Modest Defense of English Catholics* (1584), 79, 89 *seq.*

the conference upon the lawfulness of tolerating the queen's mass, but the judgment which he delivered upon the general question, grounded as it was rather upon common political principles than upon religious dogma, has been thought worthy of record by historians.[29] "I was," he said, "in the university of Bononia in the year of our Lord 1553, where in the place of the Black Friars of the same town, I saw this conclusion following set forth in their General Assembly, reasoned and determined:

> Principes omnes, tam fupremi quam inferiores, poffunt et debeent reformari vel deponi, per eos per quos eliguntur, confirmantur vel admittuntur ad officium, quoties a fide praestita subditis per juramentum deficiunt. Quoniam relatio juramenti fubditorum et principum mutua eft, et utrinque aequo jure fervanda et reformanda, juxta legem et conditionem juramenti ab utraque parte facti.

That is,

> All rulers, be they supreme or be they inferior, may and ought to be reformed and deposed by those by whom they are chosen, confirmed or admitted to their office, as often as they break their promise made by oath to their subjects because the prince is no less bound to subjects than subjects are to princes. And, therefore, it ought to be kept and reformed equally according to the law and condition of the oath which is made of either party.
>
> This proposition, my lords, I heard sustained and

[29] Laing's *Knox*, vol. ii., 456; Calderwood, vol.

> concluded, as I have said, in a most notable auditory. The sustainer was a learned man, Thomas de Finola, rector of the university, a famous man in that country, Magister Vincentius de Placentia affirmed the assertion to be most true and certain agreeable both with the law of God and man. The occasion of the disputation was a certain disorder and tyranny attempted by the pope's governours who began to make innovations in the country against the laws formerly established alleging themselves not to be subject to such laws by reason that they were not constituted of the people but by the pope who was king of that country and, therefore, that having full commission and authority from the pope they might alter and change statutes and ordinances of the country without all consent of the people. Against this their usurped tyranny the learned and the people opposed themselves openly. When all the reasons which the pope's governors did allege were heard and confuted, the pope himself was fain to take up the controversy and to promise that he not only should keep the liberty of the people, but also that he should neither abrogate any law or statute nor make any new law without their own consent. Therefore, my vote and conscience is that princes are not only bound to keep laws and promises to their subjects, but also that if they fail, they may be justly deposed for the band betwixt the prince and the people is reciproce.

Here, writes Knox, "a clawback of the corrupt court" interposed: "You tell us what was done in Bononia. We are in a kingdom, they are in a commonwealth."

To which Craig replied, "that in a kingdom no less care should be taken to prevent the violation of the law than in a commonwealth, and the more so, for the tyranny of monarchs is more hurtful to the subjects than the misgovernment of magistrates, who are changed from year to year."

The meeting broke up without arriving at any practical result. Knox, who reports the proceedings at length in his *History*, candidly admits that "after this time the ministers who were called precise were holden by the courtiers as monsters."

Advancing age and altered circumstances may have had, at a later period, a modifying influence upon the opinions entertained by Craig on the relations of subjects to their rulers, but as long, at least, as he was within range of the influence of Knox, the two men acted in the closest alliance. The suspicion which attaches to Knox of a knowledge and approval of the plot to assassinate David Riccio lies equally against his colleague. Their names appear together at the bottom of the list of "such as were at the death of Davy and privy thereto," sent by the Earl of Bedford and Randolph to Cecil, March 21, 1566, twelve days after the murder took place. Cecil's correspondents showed themselves intimately acquainted with the whole conspiracy and were by no means hostile witnesses against the "preachers" whom they implicate in it. The documents bearing on the matter are given by Patrick Fraser Tytler.[30] All the arguments which, in the belief of that historian, go to confirm the evidence of the list referred to, may not appear equally cogent to others. It does not follow, because the assassins were for the most part intimate friends of Knox and not accustomed to act except under his guidance that they would have consulted him upon this delicate point. Their seeling may have been similar to that of the Nuncio of Paris who, in an analogous case, when announcing to the Cardinal of Como the plan of the Guises for the assassination of Elizabeth, writes that he will not tell it to Gregory XIII, for though he believed "the Pope would be glad that God should punish in any way whatever that enemy of His, still it would be unfitting that His Vicar should procure it by these means."[31] The inference which is drawn from the hurried flight of Knox upon the failure of the intended issue of the plot may also be pressed too far in proof of his connection with it. But inasmuch as, while Knox was in hiding, his colleague remained at his post, the fact must be allowed to tell in

---

[30] Vol. vii.., 353-362.

[31] *Letters and Memorials of Cardinal Allen*, London, 1882, xlvii.

favor of Craig's courage, if not of his innocence.[32] On the worst supposition it is not to be thought that these men would have acted against their consciences. If their standard of morality was low, their conduct gave proof of their religious earnestness. "The slaughter of that villain Davie" was in their eyes doubtless "a just act and worthy of all praise."[33] He was doing his worst to set up again an "idolatrous worship," far more intolerable to them than any mere political tyranny. It was the duty of the magistrate, so they thought, to put to death such an enemy of the truth and destroyer of souls and if the offender could not be reached by the ordinary processes of law, the duty of executing the divine command might fall upon any individual who possessed the opportunity and the power. If it is an exaggeration to say that similar views were universally prevalent at the time, they were at least entertained *mutatis mutandis* by high authorities of the most opposite religious creeds.

In the spring of 1567 Craig became involved in a contest with Mary and James Hepburn, 4th Earl of

---

[32] That he braved some danger in Edinburgh is evident from a letter of Sir John Forster, who writes to Cecil that on the 8th of May 1566, a soldier of the Queen of Scots struck at Craig with his dagger as he was sitting in the church. *Cal. State Papers*, Foreign Series, 1566-8, No. 385.

[33] Laing's *Knox*, vol. i., 235.

Bothwell, which added greatly to his renown. Knox had obtained six months leave of absence in England and Craig was consequently left the only parochial minister in Edinburgh. Darnley had been slain on the 9th of February. Shortly afterwards Mary consented to marry Bothwell, who thereupon obtained a divorce from his wife (May 7), and at once took steps for the celebration of his marriage with the queen. Mr. Thomas Hepburn called upon Craig in the queen's name to publish the banns. The minister, on the ground of the common rumor that the queen was under restraint, demanded to see her Majesty's handwriting. On the morrow, therefore, Sir John Bellenden, the Justice-Clerk, brought a letter signed by Mary declaring "she was neither ravished nor yet retained in captivity." Craig, however, insisted that such a marriage could only be solemnised in defiance of the laws of the General Assembly, that he could neither perform the ceremony nor approve of it, but he was ready to give his reasons either to the parties themselves if they would hear him, or to the Kirk. After much consultation he was summoned before Bothwell and the Council. He has left on record a full account of the transaction in his *Expurgation*, entered among the acts of the General

Assembly.[34]

> I laid to his charge (wrote Craig) the law of adultery, the law of ravishing, the suspicion of collusion betwixt him and his wife, the sudden divorcement and proclaiming within the space of four days, and last, the suspicion of the king's death, which her marriage would confirm. But he answered nothing to my satisfaction, wherefore, after many exhortations, I protested that I could but declare my mind publicly to the kirk. Therefore upon Sunday, after I had declared what they had done, and how they would proceed whether we would or not, I took heaven and earth to witness that I abhorred and detested that marriage, because it was odious and slanderous to the world; and seeing that the best part of the realm did approve it, either by flattery or by their silence, I desired the faithful to pray earnestly that God would turn it to the comfort of this realm.

Upon the Tuesday following he was again called before the Council, and accused of passing beyond the bounds of his commission, but the reprimand had no effect upon the intrepid minister, who on Wednesday once more accompanied the proclamation with his indignant protest.

The marriage took place on the 15th May and was blessed by Adam Bothwell, the bishop of Orkney, who had joined the Reformed Church. "If there is a good work to be done," remarks Knox,[35] "a bishop must do it. Here

---

[34] *Book of the Universal Kirk*, 115; Calderwood, vol. ii., 394.

[35] *History of the Reformation*, ed. Laing, vol. ii., 555.

mark the difference betwixt this worthy minister, Mr. Craig, and this base bishop." In the General Assembly, held on 25th December following, the bishop was for this and other faults suspended. Even Craig had been by some blamed for too great compliance, but after hearing his defence, the Assembly ordered it to be inserted in their minutes, to "show all persons hereafter Mr. Craig's good judgment and proceedings in that business."

During the regency of Murray, Craig took an active part in settling the affairs of the Church. But the civil war which followed the assassination of the regent was a trying time for an Edinburgh minister, Kirkaldy of Grange held the castle and town for the queen, while Knox thundered at him from the pulpit of St. Giles. On May 8, 1571, the Reformer, being at last persuaded by Craig and his friends that if violence were offered to him, "the blood which might be shed in his defense would be required by God at his hands," consented to leave the city, and took himself to St. Andrews, Craig had himself risked the anger of Kirkaldy by refusing to read from the pulpit a written message sent by him in rebuke of Knox, but he was generaly less aggressive in speech and more inclined to seek peace in compromise than his companion. He, therefore, was able to continue his ministry without fear.

His conciliatory disposition even drew upon him the censures of his own party. On Sunday, May 13, he preached a sermon in which

> he lamented there was no neutral man to make agreement betwixt the two parties, seeing whatsoever party shall be overthrown, the country shall be brought to ruin. . . . By such speeches (says Calderwood) he offended many, because he made the cause of both parties alike.[36]

At the same time the Convention of the Kirk was being held at Leith, and at his suggestion a deputation was appointed to wait upon the queen's friends at the castle with a view of coming to some terms of peace. The three deputies named were Craig, Gilbert Wynram, and Andrew Hay.

An account of the conference which they held with Maitland, Sir James Balsour, Kirkaldy, and the Duke of Chatelherault, is given in Bannatynes *Memoriah* (pp. 125-132), apparently from a narrative by Craig himself. It presents some striking contrasts to the discussion which took place in 1564. The course of events has reversed the political positions of the chief speakers. Craig is now on the side of constituted authority, while Maitland is called upon to defend what his opponent has ground for

[36] Vol. iii., 75.

stigmatising as rebellion. The minister, therefore, in meeting the charge of inconsistency, is careful to draw a distinction between matters of religious and civil policy.

> If a wicked religion enters in (he argues), how long soever it has continued, or by whatsoever authority it has been established, it ought incontinently to be rejected, but it is otherwise in the civil polity. For though the established authority of kings and princes be established (as he seems to think it generally is) by violence and tyranny, yet once established, it ought to be obeyed, much more so when the ground of that authority is lawful, reasonable, and godly.

He pressed his adversaries in turn with their inconsistency, seeing that they had all been the chief instruments in setting up that authority which they now rejected and intimated in very plain terms that those who were there present were creating disturbances in the state merely "to cloak cruel murders," and to escape punishment for their complicity in the death of Darnley. There was apparently something in Craig's character and bearing which enabled him to give utterance to such blunt speeches without risk of exasperating his antagonists. On this occasion, as the conference broke up, we are told everyone rose from his place with a smile. But the brethren in Edinburgh were hard to please. They probably misunderstood his peaceful inclinations and judged that he "sweyed over meikle ta the sword-hand." They agreed to part and in August 1572, before Knox's return to Edinburgh, we find the town petitioning the General Assembly for assistance, as it was at that moment destitute of ministers.[37] Craig was translated in that year to Montrose, and, after a short ministry there, he was appointed by the General Kirk to Aberdeen, August 6, 1574.

At Aberdeen, Craig passed six years of incessant activity on a stipend of £16, 13s. 4d. He was appointed commissioner for visiting the province of Aberdeen in 1575 and was employed in similar functions in 1576 and 1578.[38] He was a member of twelve out of thirteen Assemblies and in October 1576 he was elected moderator for a second time. It was during this period that the controversy was carried on concerning the lawfulness of the episcopal office. The question was debated in August 1575 by a committee appointed for the purpose, in which Craig, with Andrew Melville and James Lawson, was to take the negative side. Their report in condemnation of the order was approved in all points in the following year, and in 1581 bishops were utterly abolished. Craig had also a hand in the drawing up of the *Second Book of Discipline*

---

37 Bannatyne's *Memorials*; Calderwood, vol. iii., 223.
38 Fafti Eccles. Scot., Pt. vi., 462.

which was agreed upon in the Assembly of 1578. It was during his ministry here that he prepared his first, or longer, Catechism, as in the preface to the work he reminds "the Professors of Christ's Evangel at New Aberdeen" that it was for their sake chiefly that he "toook pains first to gather this brief summary" and he now (July 1581) in setting it out and making it common to others, recommends the same to them again in special as a token of his goodwill and a memorial of his doctrine and earnest labors bestowed upon them for the space of six years.

In the fortieth Assembly, held at Edinburgh, July 7, 1579, among certain articles presented to the king was a petition that, as "his Highness" house is too great a charge for any one man, his Majesty would be pleased to nominate any one of the best-gifted in the kingdom to be adjoined colleague to Mr. John Duncanson, and in the following year, July 12, it appears that "the king by his letters nominates Mr. John Craig to be his minister, for which the Assembly blessed the Lord and praised the king for his zeal."[39] Meanwhile, in view of his appointment as Royal Chaplain, Craig had left Aberdeen, September 14, 1579, "with his wife, children, and whole house."[40]

---

[39] Row, 67, 68.
[40] Fafti Eccles. Scot., Pt. vi., 462.

Craig had not long entered upon his new office, when the country was suddenly and seriously alarmed by the discovery of certain intrigues of the papal party which threatened the security of the reformed kirk and the peace of the kingdom. The Duke of Lennox, who was in league with the Guises and the pope, and in whom the Catholics put the greatest reliance, had recently come into Scotland and was gaining considerable influence over the young king. It was even believed that a number of men, Catholics at heart, had received dispensations from the pope to simulate Protestantism, to frequent the church services and receive the sacrament according to the reformed rites, in order the more secretly to carry out their designs. That some extraordinary efforts were being made on the part of Rome to recover her lost ground, both in England and Scotland, was evident, and, to meet the insidious form in which they appeared, Craig, at the suggestion of the king, drew up "A Short and General Confession of the True Christian Faith and Religion According to God's Word and Acts of our Parlaments." This powerful and indignant protest against every doctrine, rite, and ceremony then considered as distinctive of the Roman Church, is perhaps the most remarkable and characteristic document which ever emanated from the church of Scotland. This "King's

Confession," or "National Covenant" as it was afterwards called, was signed by James and his household January 28, 1580-1.[41] Underneath the royal signature, at the top of the column on the left hand, stands that of John Craig. At the head of the central column of names is the signature of the false Duke of Lennox himself. As "a touchstone to try and discern Papists from Protestants" it ought hardly to have been unsuccessful. It is difficult to understand how such a paper could have been signed by any one with the slightest inclination towards or respect for Roman Catholic teaching.

On the 2nd of March, in the same year, the king charged "all commissioners and ministers to desire the same confession of their parishioners and to proceed against the refusers according to our laws and order of the kirk, etc." In 1585 it was ordained that all persons graduating at a university should subscribe it. A copy of the confession (with the omission of some sentences) prefixed to the Book of Laureations for that purpose, is still preserved at the college in Edinburgh, and to John Craig was accorded the honor of again signing his name at the top of the list.

---

[41] A facsimile of the original with its signatures is given in the National Manuscripts of Scotland, vol. iii.

From time to time this confession, says Row, "in days of espied defection was renewed, the Kirk acknowledging that to be the principal mean, by the blessing of God for the preventing of and reclaiming from apostasy and backsliding."[42] It was again signed by the king and his household in February 1587-8; it was solemnly renewed by all sorts of persons in the year 1590 by a new ordinance of Council at the desire of the General Assembly and once more in 1595. It formed the basis of the National Covenant of 1688, when to the original text was added an abjuration of episcopacy and a recital of all the Acts of Parliament passed in favor of the Reformation and as thus embodied it was subscribed by King Charles II. at Speymouth, June 23, 1650, and at Scone, Jan. 1, 1651.

In October 1581 Craig was once more elected moderator of the Assembly. Meanwhile the threatened interference of the Catholic powers in favor of Mary and the old religion had assumed a more serious aspect. The bold counter move made by the Earl of Gowrie and his associates in seizing the person of the king, in order to place him beyond the reach of Lennox and Arran, was loudly applauded by the General Assembly and Craig, with two other ministers, was commissioned to intimate their

---

[42] *History of the Kirk*, 78.

approbation of the proceeding and to require from the king his own judgment upon the matter.[43] Craig, moreover, made use of his opportunity, as the king's minister, to read the royal prisoner some severe lessons from the pulpit. He rebuked him so sharply (September 19, 1582) for having issued a proclamation which was considered offensive to the clergy, that the king wept, and complained that this might at least have been said to him in private.[44] When James, in June 1588, recovered his liberty, and the Raid of Ruthven was declared to have been treasonable, Melville, with many ministers and noblemen who had been compromised, fled into England. Craig, as usual, did not stir.

In the Parliament of May 1584 James had his revenge for the raid by the passing of the "Black Acts," in which episcopacy was virtually restored and the royal authority declared supreme in all causes and over all persons. The acts were a sore trial to Craig. He resolutely denounced them in his sermons and was in consequence on the 24th of August summoned, with some of his brethren, before the council to answer for his conduct. There was a stormy scene. Arran asked, "how dare they fault with the acts of

[43] Spottiswood, vol. ii., 293.
[44] Calderwood, vol. iii., 670.

Parliament."

"We do and shall find fault" said Craig, "with everything that is repugnant to the word of God."

Arran in a rage sprang to his feet and swore he would shave their heads and pare their nails and make an example of them. They were charged to appear again before the king and council at Falkland on the 4th of September. They obeyed, and, as Calderwood relates,[45] "there was some hot conference betwixt Mr. Craig and the bishop of St. Andrews in the king's presence." Arran gave utterance to more "rough speeches" and on Craig reminding him that "there were men set up higher than he that have been brought low," answered derisively that he would make of "a false friar a true prophet" and, falling on his knees, in childish mockery cried, "See how I am humbled."

"Well, well" said Craig, "mock on as you please. God sees and require it at your hands that you thus trouble his church unless you repent." So Hume of Godscroft reports the minister's speech.[46] Calderwood puts into his mouth words which may be taken as a prophecy that Arran should one day "be cast down from the high horse of his pride," and the historian thinks he finds their fulfilment in

---

[45] Vol. iv., 198.

[46] *History of the House of Douglas and Angus*, vol. ii., 337.

the fact that a few years later the earl was thrown from his horse and slain by James Douglas of Parkhead and his body eaten by dogs.

Further pressure was now put upon the clergy. Craig was interdicted from preaching, and, as two of the ordinary ministers of Edinburgh had fled the country, and the third had been removed elsewhere, the city was for some weeks without a preacher. In August all ministers had been ordered by Parliament to sign an act of submission to the late ordinances and to promise obedience to the bishops appointed by the crown under pain of losing their beenefices.[47] The threat was not an idle one and several ministers who refused subscription were deprived of their stipends. The king further declared that they should be banished from the country. [48]

At this crisis, Craig unexpectedly intervened as the leader and spokesman of a moderate party holding an intermediate position between the favorers of episcopacy on the one hand and the extreme presbyterians, led by Melville, on the other.[49] It has been suggested by some that the bond might be signed with a safe conscience if a clause

---

[47] Grub's *Eccles. Hift.*, vol. ii., 235.
[48] Calderwood, vol. iv., 211.
[49] Register of the Privy Council, vol. iv., 37 – *note* by Professor Mason.

were inserted, "as far as the word of God permits." Arran had contemptuously rejected the proposed compromise, but the king, under the influence of Craig, was less unmanageable. A paper was drawn up and presented to James by nine members, including Craig, who is said to have been its author, in which, while expressing the most affectionate loyalty to the king, they respectfully urge their objections to the acts in question, but offer to subscribe a general obedience to the laws with the conditional clause above mentioned. The king accepted the olive branch, and accordingly about the end of December, Craig and Duncanson, the two ministers of the king's household, and John Brand, minister of Holyrood House, subscribed; and Craig wrote a circular letter urging his brethren to do the same. In this letter he protested that, according to the understanding they had come to with the king, their subscription was not to be taken as an allowance of the Act of Parliament nor of the state of the bishops, but simply as a testimony of obedience to his Majesty so that "no man can refuse the same who loves God or the quietness of the kirk for commonweal" The king added a postscript, declaring that the letter was written with his knowledge.

Craig's example was immediately followed by Erskine

of Dun, who used his great influence in the north on the side of his old friend, and finally by a large number of ministers. This conciliatory action was so far successful that within a short time subscription was no longer insisted upon and Melville and the other exiles were able to return to their country. The conduct of Craig, which lays him open to the charge of vacillation and weakness, naturally excited the indignation of many of his contemporaries. It is said that his spirit was broken by the threats held over him, but there is no appearance of him having been influenced by any meaner motive than his habitual love of peace and dislike of faction. Mr. Scott, the biographer of the Scottish Reformers, ventures to call the proceeding "the boldest action in his political conduct."[50]

That a change had taken place at this time in Craig's political views cannot, however, be doubted. Some of the exiled clergy whom he now branded with the name of "peregrine ministers," on their return to their pulpits, inveighed against the subscribers and their leader. Stung by these reproaches, and by some words by James Gibson of Pencaitland in particular, Craig preached a famous sermon before the Parliament at Linlithgow in justification of the course he had adopted. Taking for his text the verse of the

[50] *Edinburgh Christian Instructor*, vol. iii., 223.

82nd Psalm, "God sits among the assembly of the gods," he apparently unsaid all that he had learned at Bologna and upheld at the conference with Maitland thirty years before. The sermon is remarkable as having been the subject of an exceedingly interesting discussion between the Earl of Angus, one of the refugee lords, and David Hume of Godscroft, who reports the argument, in which he took a very able part, at some length in his *History of the House of Douglas and Angus*.[51] Hume takes the conclusion of the sermon to be in short "Obedience to Tyrants, Impunity to Tyrants," and from his analysis we learn that Craig inferred from the examples of Scripture, that, "as the people of God are commanded to obey Nebuchadnezzar who was a tyrant, therefore all tyrants should be obeyed; that as David did not slay Saul, therefore no man may put him out, though his tyranny be never so great." Neither passive obedience nor the divine right of kings was doctrine of the minister of St. Giles in 1564.[52]

The remainder of Craig's life was passed undisturbed

---

[51] Vol. ii. p. 383 ſeq.; also Calderwood, vol. iv., 466.

[52] Craig and Duncanson have been accused (Stephen's *History of the Church of Scotland*) of disobedience to the king's command that prayers should be publicly offered for the preservation of his mother. This is a mistake. Spottiswood distinctly states that the king's ministers and David Lyndsay of Leith "gave obedience." Compare M'Crie's *Melville*, 131.

by ecclesiastical or political strife. His name still frequently occurs in the minutes of the General Assembly and at its request he composed in 1591 the "Form of Examination Before Communion," already referred to, which was in use in all schools and families until 1648 when it was superseded by the Westminster Catechisms. To the same year belongs an incident related by Calderwood, which is characteristic both of the king and his minister. The failure of the attack made upon Holyrood House by Francis Stewart, Earl of Bothwell, was the subject of a sermon preached by Craig before the king on December 29, in which, referring to a number of murderous outrages which had recently been allowed to go unpunished, he reminded his Majesty that as he "had lightly regarded the many bloody shirts presented to him by his subjects craving justice, so God in his providence had made a noise of crying and fore-hammers to come to his own doors." The king who was ruffled at this frankness of speech, addressed the congregation and said, that "if he had thought his servant would have dealt after that manner with him, he would not have suffered him so long in his house."[53]

---

[53] Calderwood, vol. v., 321. There had been a proceffion of men expofing the bloody fhirts of the victims through the ftreets of

Two years later, April 24, 1598, we find James desiring the General Assembly to nominate "six of the discreetest of the ministry that he might make choice of two of them to serve in his house in respect of Mr. Craig, his decrepit age." No action, however, seems to have been taken in the matter at this time, and in 1594 the old man was still able to take an active part in a committee of the General Assembly.[54] In June 1595, the king sent another message, that "as Mr. John Craig is awaiting what hour it shall please God to call him and is altogether unable to serve any longer and his Majesty minds to place John Duncanson with the prince, therefore his Highness desires an ordinance to be made, granting him any two ministers he shall choose."[55] But nevertheless Craig nominally retained his office until his death, which took place peaceably in the eighty-ninth year of his age, at Edinburgh, on the 12th of December 1600. During the last five years he seems to have lived privately at home, taking no part in public services.[56] Spottiswoode, the historian, was appointed one of his immediate successors as minister to the king's household in the following year. The Testament of John

---

the city, *ibid.*, 256.

[54] Calderwood, vol. v., 321.

[55] *Ibid.*, 368.

[56] Spottiswood, vol. iii., 94. M'Crie's *Melville*, vol. ii., 223.

Craig, made 17th May 1595, is still extant among the Commissary Records of Edinburgh. The inventory of his effects amounts to £222, 13s, 4d., and the debts owing to him at the time of his death to £1100. He nominated his wife, Marion Smaill, and his son William, his sole executors, and enjoins them in the administration of the trust to seek the advice of Mr. Thomas Craig, Advocate.[57] He requests his "small children" to remain in household with their mother until the time of their marriage "with parties honest," and with their mother's consent. He leaves all his books to his son William, and 100 merks to the Hospital of Edinburgh.[58] The date of his marriage has not been ascertaind nor the number of his children, but, as has been seen, he left Aberdeen at the end of 1579 with "wife and children." The baptism of William is entered under date of October 9, 1575, in the Registry of Births at Aberdeen, now in the Register House, Edinburgh. According to Calderwood, "Mr. John Craig's son, a young boy," took part in the pageant prepared for the entertainment of Anne of Denmark, on her entry into Edinburgh on the 19th of May 1590, and "made a short

---

[57] Sir Thomas died 26 Feb. 1608, in his 70th year.

[58] Reg. of Testaments. *Comm. Of Edinb.* Vol. 35. The editor is indebted for this information to the kindness of Mr. Thomas Dickson of the Register House.

oration" to her Majesty. This is, no doubt, William himself, "a very able and gracious boy" says Crawford, who took his degree at the University Edinburgh in 1598, and whose name already appears under the date 1587 among the signatures attached the copy of the "King's Confession" preserved at the college. He was appointed professor of philosophy in 1599, and in the following year, that of his father's death, he resigned his office and went into France, where he became professor of divinity at Saumur. After a few years he returned to Scotland and died, November 1616, "much regretted," at his own house in Blackfriars Wynd, Edinburgh.[59]

The "Shorte Summary" is memorable as having been the first, or, if we include the briefer "Form of Examination" by the same author, the only catechism in the vernacular of purely Scottish origin, which came into common use in the reformed kirk. Its predecessor, and the immediate successor of Archbishop Hamilton's *Roman Catholic Catechism*, so called, was an English translation of Calvin's *Catechism*, first printed at Geneva in 1556, and approved in the first *Book of Discipline*, 1560, "as the most

---

[59] Crawford, *Hist. of the University*, 39; Dalzel, *Hist of the University*, vol. ii., 7.

perfect that ever yet was used in the Kirk." But it does not appear to have been printed in Scotland till 1564, when an edition appeared at Edinburgh from the press of Robert Lekprevik. The next in order of time which met with any general acceptance was this catechism of John Craig. There is no record, however, of its having had the formal approval of the General Assembly such as was accorded to the little "Form of Examination" printed ten years later (between July 1591 and May 1592), after four editions of the larger work had already been published. Almost simultaneously with the later or shorter catechism of Craig, an English translation of the Heidelberg or Palatine Catechism was printed at Edinburgh (1591), claiming on the title-page to be "Now authorized by the King's Majesty for the Use of Scotland." Dr. Bonar, who gives it a place in his *Collection*, says that he has not been able to find any Act of Assembly authorising it, nor any reference to it in the history of the Church. All these were finally superseded by the Westminster Catechisms approved in 1648.

In the matter of doctrine, Craig's *Catechism* contains nothing distinctive. Its theology is the purest Calvinism. Although in extent of matter it is considerably longer than the present "Shorter Catechism," it is less abstruse and its language is simpler. In form it differs from the

Westminster Catechisms chiefly by introducing into the body of the work the so-called Apostle's Creed which is made the text of a large portion of the theological teaching. The author himself tells us that he has studied "to be plain, simple, short and profitable." He has of set purpose to "abstained from all curious and hard questions," and has put both questions and answers into as few words as possible, "for the ease of children and common people." In the opinion of competent judges the work was admirably adapted for its purpose.

The edition of the "Confession of Faith" appended to the *Catechism* is interesting, as, if not the first printed copy of that famous document, it was at least published by the author himself within a few months of the signing of the original.[60] It differs verbally in a few instances from the original manuscript, and is rendered more emphatic by dividing the long enumeration of papal errors into separate clauses. The very characteristic supplement added in confirmation of its principles does not appear elsewhere.

[60] It may be well, however, to note a strange error in the date at the head of the *Confession*, which should be January 28, not 20, as printed in the text of 1581. The edition of 1597 gives "20 of June."

A S H O RT E SVMME OF THE WHO-LE CATECHISME WHEREIN

the Queftion is proponed and anfwered
in few wordes, for the greater eafe
of the commoune peo-
ple and children.

Gathered by M. IOHNE CRAIG,
Minifter of GOD'S WORDE to
the Kings M.

IOHNE. XVII.
**This is Lyfe Eternal, to Knowe the
Onely verie** GOD, **& whome thou
hast sent** IESVS CHRIST.

IMPRINTED AT EDIN-
Burgh, by Henrie Charteris
ANNO, M.D, LXXXI.

Cum Priuilegio Regali

A SHORT SUMMARY OF THE WHOLE CATECHISM WHEREIN THE QUESTION IS PUT AND ANSWERED IN FEW WORDS FOR GREATER EASE OF THE COMMON PEOPLE AND CHILDREN (1581)

BY

JOHN CRAIG

The following is a modernized version of John Craig's longer catechism in its entirety including the *National Covenant* (or *King's Confession*) later attached to the original document. Craig also wrote a preface and a letter to the reader at the beginning of the document.

THE CONTENTS OF THIS BOOK DIVIDED INTO TEN PARTS

To the Professors of Christ's Gospel at New Aberdeen, Master John Craig wishes the perpetual comfort and increase of the Holy Spirit to the end of their battle.

It is not unknown to some of you (dear brethren in the Lord) that for your fake chiefly, I took pains first to gather this brief *Summary*. Therefore, willing now to set it out and make it common to others I thought it good to recommend the same to you again in special as a token of my goodwill towards you all and as a memorial of my doctrine and earnest labors bestowed among you and upon that country for the space of six years. Wherefore desiring to hear of your profit and fruits of my labors I cannot, but of very love and duty, exhort you, not only to take this my labor in good part but also to use it aright least it be a witness against you in the day of the Lord. It shall be very comfortable and fruitful to you if you cause this short summary to be often and diligently read in your house: for hereby you yourselves, your children, and servants may profit more and more in the principal points of your salvation. You need to have this continual exercise in your houses, you yourselves, and I by experience can bear witness of the great and gross ignorance of some among you notwithstanding the clear light of the gospel of long was shining there. In handling of this matter, I have studied to my power to be plain, simple, short, and profitable, not looking for much to the desire and satisfaction of the learned as to the instruction and help of the ignorant. For first, I have abstained from all curious and hard questions, and next, I have brought the questions and the answers to as few words as I could, and that for the ease of children and common people, who cannot understand nor gather the substance of a long question or a long answer confirmed with many reasons. And yet if any will exercise their household in the common Catechism, (which I exhort all men to do), this my labor cannot hurt, but rather it shall be a great help to them seeing I both gather the substance of the whole Catechism in few words and also follow the same order, except a little in the beginning and in the end, where certain things are added, which all men I hope shall judge to be very profitable and necessary to be known. There are also some questions and answers interlaced in various places, but chiefly in the matter of the sacraments, which serve greatly to the great understanding of the matter in hand. But if men will be both weary to learn the cognition catechism, and also this brief summary. I cannot understand what good they will have to know the right way of their salvation. For certain, and sure it is, that the reading or rehearsing (by word) of the Belief, of the Lord's Prayer, the Law, and number of the holy sacraments, can profit nothing to salvation, without the right understanding and lively application of the same to ourselves in particular, in the which only does the true Christian faith consist. For this reason I marvel greatly of the brutishness of many, who glory in faith, and yet neither have they knowledge, nor seeling of the principal heads of our Christian faith, as their answers do testify when they are brought to any public examination. But albeit the great multitude perish in their willfull ignorance, yet I hope some shall profit by my labour, taken for the church of God, of which I judge you to be a part. Therefore take heed to yourselves and suffer no others to go before you in this spiritual exercise. For greater honor it shall be to you if others shall profit more by this brief summary then if you, seeing for your cause it was first written, taught among you and now lastly under your name come to the knowledge of others. Be not of those men, to whom all kind of good doctrine is either hard and obscure or else over base and common. For as the one has no will to learn even so the other would be hostile with some curiosity or new doctrine. If any man shall complain of my obscurity in these short answers, let him consider how hard a thing it is, to be both short and plain, or yet to satisfy all men's desire and judgment in lighter matters, then this is. Always if days be granted, I mind with the help of God, to make this summary more adequate and more plain, if the brethren shall judge it needful. In the meantime, I desire all men to take this my travail in good part, and use it to the edification of the church and the glory of our God to whom be all honor and praise forever and ever

Amen.

At Edenburgh, the xx. of July,
in the year 1581.

To the Reader,

Marvel not, gentle reader, that I alledge no authority of the scriptures nor fathers for the confirmation of this doctrine seeing my purpose is not so much to instruct our profane atheists and apostates as to put our brethren in memory of that doctrine, which they daily hear confirmed (in our ordinary teaching) by the scriptures and consent of the godly fathers.

Always if either the brethren or other would have further confirmation of this doctrine, let them read the *Institution of John Calvin* and other godly men who have written aboundantly for the defence of this doctrine according to the scriptures of God. I doubt not but good men, and such as are persuaded of the truth, will take this excuse of mine in the best part and give thanks to God for my labor taken for their comfort. But as for the godless band of atheists and apostates whom God has ordained to destruction I care not what they shall judge of this my simple writing and pains taken for the instruction of the ignorant, I would marvel greatly of the success of our doctrine which is not impugned and pursued by men to the fight of the world (of great estimation and judgment) if the same had come to pass to the prophets and apostles in their age whose doctrine and religion was most falsely impugned and cruelly persecuted by the sons of perdition. Of this we are forewarned by the apostles that men after witnessing the truth shall depart to their vomit again and become traitors and persecutors of God's truth which they professed with us. When we see this fiery trial and fearful judgment in the church, let us examine ourselves before it is too late and call to God for constancy in the truth and praise his justice in the blinding of those that in so great a light willingly and maliciously delight in darkness and blasphemy the way of righteousness. Of this sort are a variety in our nation whose blasphemous writinges come daily to our hands to the trial of our faith and constancy to the further blinding of the reprobate and their greater condemnation in the day of our Lord Jesus Christ. To whom with the Father and the Holy Spirit be all honor and praise eternally.

Amen.

1.
THE CREATION OF MAN AND HIS FIRST ESTATE OF INNOCENCE WITHOUT DEATH AND MISERY

Question. Who made man and woman?
Answer. The eternal God in his goodness.

Q. How did he make them?
A. Of an earthly body and a heavenly Spirit.

Q. In whose image did he make them?
A. In his own Image.

Q. What is the Image of God?
A. Perfect uprightness in body and soul.

Q. To what end were they made?
A. To acknowledge and serve their Maker.

Q. How should they have served him?
A. According to his holy will.

Q. How did they know his will?
A. By his works, word, and sacraments.

Q. What liberty did they have to obey his will?
A. They had free will to obey and disobey.

Q. What profit had they by their obedience?
A. They were blessed and happy in body and soul.

Q. Was this blessedness given to them only?
A. No, but it was given to them and their posterity.

Q. With what condition was it given?
A. With the condition of their obedience to God.

Q. Why was so small a commandment given?
A. To show God's gentleness and to try man's obedience.

Q. What advantage is there in knowing of his lost blessedness?
A. Hereby we know God's goodness and our ingratitude.

Q. But we cannot come to this estate again?
A. We come to better state in Christ.

Q. What should we learn of this discourse?
A. That the church was first planted, blessed and made happy through obedience to God's Word.

2.
The Miserable Fall Of Man From God And His Former Estate Under The Bondage Of Sin, Death, And All Other Kinds Of Miseries

Q. What brought them from that blessed estate?
A. Satan and their own unfaithfulness.

Q. How were they brought to that inconstancy?
A. Through familiar conference with Satan against the Word.

Q. What thing did Satan first want from them?
A. Distrust and contempt of God's Word.

Q. Why did he begin at their faith?
A. Because he knew it was their life.

Q. How could they consent to their own perdition?
A. They were deceived by the craft of Satan.

Q. What was the craft of Satan here?
A. He persuaded them that good was evil and evil was good.

Q. How could they be persuaded having the image of God?
A. They had the image but not the gift of constancy.

Q. What did they lose through their fall?
A. The favor and image of God with the use of the creatures.

Q. What succeeded the loss of the favor and image of God?
A. The wrath of God and original sin.

Q. What is original sin?
A. The corruption of our whole nature.

Q. How does this sin come to us?
A. By natural propagation from our first parents.

Q. What are the fruits of this sin?
A. All other sins which we commit.

Q. What is the punishment of this sin?
A. Death of body and soul with all other miseries.

Q. What else followed upon this sin?
A. A curse upon the creatures and our banishment from the use of them.

Q. But the very wicked use them abundantly.
A. That is with testimony of an evil conscience.

Q. Were these pains too great for eating the forbidden fruit?
A. Their sin was not simply eating the fruit.

Q. What was their sin then?
A. Infidelity, pride, and open rebellion to God.

Q. How can that be proven?
A. They consented to Satan's lies, mistrusted God's Word, and fought to be equal with God.

Q. Why are we punished for their sin?
A. We are punished for our own sin seeing we are all in them standing and falling with them.

Q. In what estate is all their posterity?
A. Under the same bondage of sin.

Q. What natural freedom do we have?
A. We have freedom to sin and offend our God.

Q. Have we not power to serve and please God?
A. None at all, until we be called and sanctified.

Q. Have we lost our minds and wills?
A. No, but we have lost a right mind and a right will.

Q. Natural men may do many good deeds?
A. Yet they cannot please God without faith.

Q. Why did God suffer this fall of man?
A. For the declaration of his mercy and justice.

Q. Explain that.
A. By his mercy the chosen are delivered and the rest are punished by his justice.

3.

THE CALLING OF MAN AGAIN TO REPENTANCE AND HIS THIRD ESTATE IN JESUS CHRIST AND HOW HE SHOULD HONOR HIS REDEEMER IN FOUR WAYS

Q. Who called our parents to repentance?
A. Only God in his infinite mercy.

Q. What did they do when he called them?
A. They hid and excused themselves.

Q. But it was foolishness to fly from God?
A. Such is the foolishness of all his posterity.

Q. How were they converted to God?
A. By the almighty power of God's Spirit.

Q. How did the Spirit work their conversion?
A. He printed the promise of mercy in their hearts.

Q. What was their promise of mercy?
A. Victory in the seed of the woman against the Serpent.

Q. What is the seed of the woman?
A. Jesus Christ, God and man.

Q. How was his posterity converted to God?
A. By the same Spirit and promise.

Q. May we understand and receive the promise by ourselves?
A. No more than blind and dead men may see and walk.

Q. What more is required for our conversion to God?
A. He must enlighten our minds, and mollify our hearts, that we may understand, receive, and retain his promise.

Q. But Adam did know his sin and God's voice.
A. Yet that knowledge did not bring him to repentance.

Q. What was the cause of that?
A. For the seeling of mercy was not yet given to him.

Q. What then are knowledge, calling, accusation, and conviction?
A. A way to desperation if mercy is not apprehended.

Q. What if mercy is offered and apprehended?
A. Then these things are the beginning of our repentance.

Q. How did Adam and his posterity receive the promise?
A. Only through their own lively faith in Christ.

Q. What was their faith?
A. A sure confidence in God's mercy through Christ to come.

Q. Who wrought this faith in them above nature?
A. God's Spirit through the preaching of the promise.

Q. What is this promise called in the Scripture?
A. The gospel or glad tidings of salvation.

Q. Then the gospel was preached in paradise?
A. No doubt and also the Law.

Q. What need was there of them both?
A. By the Law they were accused and humbled and through the gospel comforted and delivered.

Q. What, then, was the Law and the gospel?
A. Instruments of God's Spirit to the salvation of man.

Q. In what did their salvation consist?
A. In the remission of their sins and reparation of God's image.

Q. What followed upon the repairing of that image?
A. A continual battle both within and without.

Q. From where does this battle proceed?
A. From the two contrary images in mankind.

Q. What are these images?
A. The image of God and the image of the Serpent.

Q. What will be the end of this battle?
A. Victory to the seed of the woman and destruction to the seed of the Serpent in mankind.

Q. Was all Adam's posterity delivered and restored?
A. No, but only they who believed the promise.

Q. To what end were these delivered?
A. To acknowledge and serve their God.

Q. In what did their service chiefly stand?
A. In the exercise of faith and repentance.

Q. What rule did he give them for this purpose?
A. His most holy Word and Scriptures.

Q. What was contained in the word given to them?
A. The Law, the gospel, and the sacraments.

Q. What did the Law do for them?
A. It showed their sin and the right way to know and serve God.

Q. What did the gospel do?
A. It offered to them mercy in Christ.

Q. What did the sacraments do for them?
A. They helped their faith in the promises of God.

Q. Was this order kept in the Old Testament?
A. No doubt, as Moses and the prophets bear witness.

Q. What should we gather of this discourse?
A. That the church was ever grounded upon the Word of God.

Q. What follows upon the corruption of the Word?
A. The corruption of the true religion and the church at all times.

Q. Was the faith and religion of the Fathers different from our faith?
A. Not in substance but in certain circumstances.

Q. What is the substance?
A. The covenant of Jesus Christ.

Q. Why do we call it the Old Testament?
A. In respect of the obscure shadows and figures joined with the doctrine and religion.

Q. What profit came to the Fathers at all times through faith?
A. By this way only they were blessed and happy.

Q. Wherein did the unhappiness of men stand?
A. In the false knowledge of the true God.

Q. Are we in the same miserable state?
A. No doubt, as our Master testifies.

Q. When do we know God aright?
A. When we give to him his due honor.

Q. What are the chief points of his due honor?
A. Faith, obedience, prayer, and thanks with their fruits.

4.

THE FIRST PART OF GOD'S HONOR IS FAITH. HERE THE BELIEF AND FAITH IS DECLARED

Q. Why is faith given the first place?
A. Because it is the mother of all the rest.

Q. What does faith work in us?
A. It moves us to put our whole confidence in God.

Q. How may we be moved to do this?
A. By the knowledge of his power and goodness.

Q. But we are unworthy and guilty?
A. Therefore we apprehend his promise in Christ.

Q. Which are the principal heads of his promise?
A. They are contained in our belief called the Apostle's Creed.

Q. Repeat the belief or Creed of the Apostles.
A. I believe in God the Father Almighty, maker of heaven and earth. And in Jesus Christ his only Son our Lord, who was conceived by the Holy Spirit: born of the virgin Mary, suffered under Pontius Pilate, was crucified, dead, and buried, he descended into hell.

He rose again the third day from the dead. He ascended into heaven and sits at the right hand of God the Father Almighty. From thence he shall come to judge the quick and the dead.

I believe in the Holy Spirit.

The holy Church universal, the communion of saints, the forgiveness of sins, the rising again of the bodies, and life everlasting.

Q. Why is it called the Apostle's Creed?
A. Because it agrees with their doctrine and time.

Q. How many parts is it divided?
A. Into four principal parts.

Q. What are we taught in the first part?
A. The right knowledge of God the Father.

Q. What are we taught in the second part?
A. The right knowledge of God the Son.

Q. What are we taught in the third part?
A. The right knowledge of God the Holy Spirit.

Q. What are we taught in the fourth part?
A. The right knowledge of the Church and gifts given to it.

Q. How many gods are there?
A. Only one eternal God, maker of all things.

Q. Why then do we name God three times here?
A. Because there are three distinct persons in the Godhead.

Q. Why is the Father put in the first place?
A. Because he is the fountain of all things.

Q. Why is the Son put in the second place?
A. Because he is the eternal wisdom of the Father begotten before all beginnings.

Q. Why is the Spirit put in the third place?
A. Because he is the power proceeding from the Father and the Son.

Q. Why is the church put in the fourth place?
A. Because it is the good work of these three persons.

The first part of our belief

Q. Why is it said particularly, "I believe?"
A. Because everyone should live by his own faith.

Q. Should everyone know what he believes?
A. Otherwise he does not have true faith.

Q. Are we bound to confess our faith openly?
A. Yes no doubt, when time and place do require.

Q. Is it enough to believe that there is a God?
A. No, but we must know who the true God is.

Q. Is it enough to know who the true God is?
A. No, but we must also know what he will be to us.

Q. How can we know that?
A. By his promise and works done for our comfort.

Q. What does he promise us?
A. To be our loving Father and Savior.

Q. What does this promise require of us?
A. A full trust and confidence in him.

Q. What then moves us to believe in God?
A. A sense and sealing of his Fatherly love.

Q. Why do we call him Father?
A. In respect of Christ and of ourselves.

Q. Explain that?
A. He is Christ's Father by nature and ours by grace through him.

Q. How then are we called sons of wrath?
A. In respect of our natural estate by sin.

Q. When are we assured to be his sons?
A. When we believe in his fatherly love.

Q. Why do we mention his power here?
A. To assure us that he can and will save us.

Q. What power do we mean here?
A. The power which disposes all things.

Q. What should the knowledge of this work in us?
A. Humility, confidence, and boldness.

Q. Why do we begin at his fatherly love and power?
A. Because they are the chief grounds of our faith.

Q. Explain that more plainly?
A. By these two, we are persuaded of all the rest of his promises.

Q. What is meant here by heaven and earth?
A. All the creatures in heaven and earth.

Q. Of what did he make all these creatures?
A. He made them all of nothing by his Word.

Q. Why did he do that?
A. To show his infinite power.

Q. Why, then, did he occupy six days?
A. That he might be able to better consider him in his works.

Q. Why are they put in our belief?
A. To bear witness to us of their Creator.

Q. What things do they testify of him?
A. That he is infinite in power, wisdom, and goodness.

Q. What other things do they teach us in special?
A. His fatherly care and providence for us.

Q. Who rules and keeps all things?
A. The same eternal God that made them.

Q. Who makes all these fearful alterations in nature?
A. The hand of God, either for our comfort or punishment?

Q. Who rules Satan and all his instruments?
A. Our God also by his almighty power and providence.

Q. What comfort do we have from this?
A. This comfort: nothing can hurt us without our Father's good will.

Q. What if Satan and his instruments should have freedom over us?
A. We should be then in a most miserable estate.

Q. What should his fatherly care work in us?
A. Thanks for all things that come to us.

Q. What other things should it work?
A. Boldness in our vocation against all impediments.

Q. Who rules sin which is not of God?
A. He only rules all the actions and defections that come to pass in heaven and earth.

Q. Why should we believe that?
A. Because he is God Almighty above his creatures.

Q. But sin is not a creature?
A. But he would not be the Almighty if he did not rule it.

Q. Is God a partaker of sin when he rules sin?
A. No, for he works his own good work by it.

Q. Are the wicked excused through their good works?
A. No, for they work their own evil work.

Q. Why are they not excused, seeing God's will concurs with them?
A. They mean one thing and God another.

Q. What do they mean in their actions?
A. Contempt of God and hurt of his creatures.

Q. What does God mean in using them and their sin?
A. The trial of his own or the punishment of sin.

Q. What should we learn by this discourse?
A. To fear only the Lord our God.

Q. What shall we judge of them that use familiarity with Satan?
A. They deny this first article of our belief.

Q. May we not conjure Satan to revealed secrets?
A. No, for he is the author of lies.

Q. But he oftentimes speaks the truth.
A. That is to get the greater credit in his lies.

Q. May we not remove witchcraft with witchcraft?
A. No, for that is to seek help from Satan.

The second part of our belief

Q. What do we learn in the second part?
A. The truth and justice of God in our redemption?

Q. Who is our redeemer and who redeemed us?
A. Jesus Christ who redeemed us by his death.

Q. What kind of person is he?
A. Perfect God and perfect man.

Q. Why was he both God and man?
A. That he might be a suitable mediator for us.

Q. Why was this name Jesus or Savior given only by God?
A. To assure us the better of our salvation by him.

Q. Is there any virtue in this name?
A. No, but the virtue is in the person.

Q. Why was he called "Christ," or "Anointed"?
A. He was anointed King, Priest, and Prophet for us.

Q. To what purpose do these titles serve?
A. Hereby is expressed his office and how he saved us.

Q. Explain that more plainly?
A. He saved us by his Kingdom, Priesthood, and prophecies.

Q. How can this be proved?
A. By the anointing of kings, priests, and prophets which were figures of his anointing.

Q. Was Christ anointed with material oil?
A. No, but he was anointed with the gift of the Spirit without measure.

Q. What kind of kingdom does he have?
A. It is spiritual pertaining chiefly to our souls.

Q. In what does his kingdom consist?
A. In God's Word and his Holy Spirit?

Q. What do we get by the Word and Spirit?
A. Righteousness and everlasting life.

Q. What is his priesthood?
A. An office appointed for the satisfaction of God's wrath.

Q. How did he satisfy God's wrath for us?
A. By his obedience, prayer, and everlasting sacrifice.

Q. Why is he called our only Prophet?
A. He ever was, is, and shall be the only teacher of the Church.

Q. What then were the prophets and the apostles?
A. All of them were his disciples and servants.

Q. Why were all these honorable offices given to him?
A. That by them he might deliver us from sin.

Q. Explain that particularly in these three offices.
A. By his kingly power we are free from sin, death, and hell.

Q. But we may easily fall into sin again?
A. Yet by the same power we shall rise and get the victory.

Q. The battle is very hard?
A. We do not fight in our own strength.

Q. What is our armor and strength?
A. The power and Spirit of Christ in us.

Q. What profit comes to us through his priesthood?
A. Hereby he is our mediator and we are priests also.

Q. How are we made priests?
A. By him we have freedom to enter in before God and offer up ourselves and all that we have.

Q. What kind of sacrifice is this?
A. A sacrifice of thanksgiving only.

Q. May we not offer Christ again for our sins?
A. No, for Christ cannot die again.

Q. What profit do we have from his prophecy?
A. Hereby we know most plainly his Father's will.

Q. What other profit do we have?
A. All revelations and prophecies are finished.

Q. But some things are not yet fulfilled?
A. That is true, but we speak of things pertaining to his first coming.

Q. Why was he called his only son?
A. Because he is his only son by nature.

Q. Yet he is called the first begotten among many brethren?
A. That is in respect of his communicating with us.

Q. Why is he called our Lord?
A. Because he bears rule over us and is head to man and angel.

Q. Why was he conceived by the Holy Spirit?
A. That he might be without sin and so sanctify us.

Q. What if he had been a sinner?
A. Then he could not have delivered us.

Q. Was he only made free from sin?
A. No, but he was also replenished with the Holy Spirit without measure.

Q. Why was the fullness of the Spirit given to him?
A. That he should bestow the same upon us.

Q. Why was he made man like unto us?
A. That he might die for us in our own nature.

Q. What thing followed upon his incarnation?
A. That life and righteousness is placed in our flesh.

Q. May not this life be lost as it was in Adam?
A. No, for our flesh is joined personally with the fountain of life.

Q. Then all men are sure of this life?
A. Not so, but only they which are joined with him spiritually.

Q. What then does our carnal union with Christ avail?
A. Nothing, without our spiritual union with him.

Q. What purpose does his mother's virginity serve?
A. It is a seal of his miraculous conception.

Q. Was he holy through her virginity?
A. No, seeing our whole nature is corrupted.

Q. Why is she named in our belief?
A. That we may know his tribe and family.

Q. How can that help our faith?
A. That we may know him to be the promised Savior.

Q. Of what tribe and house was he promised?
A. Of the tribe of Judah and of the house of David.

Q. How did he redeem us?
A. He suffered death for us willingly according to God's decree.

Q. Why did he suffer under the form of judgment?
A. To assure us the better that we are free from God's judgment.

Q. But the judge, Pilate, did pronounce him innocent?
A. That made greatly for our comfort.

Q. What comfort do we have by this?
A. That he died not for his own sins but for ours.

Q. But the judge meant no such thing?
A. We do not look at what he meant but what God meant by his wicked judgment.

Q. Why did he suffer upon the cross?
A. To assure us that he took our curse upon himself.

Q. What assurance do we have of this?
A. Because that kind of death was accursed of God.

Q. Was he also cursed of God?
A. No, but he sustained our curse.

Q. Was he guilty before God?
A. No, but he sustained the person of guilty men.

Q. What comfort do we have of this?
A. He removed our curse and gave to us his blessing.

Q. In what part did he suffer?
A. Both in body and soul.

Q. Why is that?
A. Because we were lost both in body and soul.

Q. What did He suffer in his soul?
A. The fearful wrath and angry face of God.

Q. What pain was that?
A. The anguish of death and pain of hell.

Q. How do we know that?
A. By his praying, sweating, and strong crying with tears.

Q. How did he sustain these pains?
A. Through faith, patience, and prayer to his Father.

Q. How do the damned sustain these pains in hell?
A. With despair and continual blasphemy.

Q. When did Christ descend to hell?
A. When he sustained these fearful pains upon the cross.

Q. Why did God punish an innocent man so grievously?
A. Because he took upon himself the burden of our sins.

Q. Was God content with his satisfaction?
A. No doubt, for he in his mercy appointed it.

Q. Was his death also necessary for our redemption?
A. Otherwise the decrees and the figures in the law had not been fulfilled.

Q. If he died for us why do we die?
A. Our death is not now a punishment for our sins.

Q. What other thing can it be?
A. It is made, through his death, a ready passage to a better life.

Q. What should we learn by all these fearful pains?
A. To know the terrible wrath of God for sin and how dearly we are bought.

Q. What comfort do we have by these sufferings of Christ our redeemer?
A. This, that the faithful members of Christ shall never suffer them.

Q. But we were oppressed by the curse of the law?
A. It is true, but Christ took it upon himself and gave us the blessing.

Q. What profit do we get in special by his death?
A. It is a sufficient and everlasting sacrifice for our sins.

Q. What does this sacrifice work perpetually?
A. It removes all things and restores all good things.

Q. Is there any priest and sacrifice for sin now?
A. None at all, for Christ has satisfied once for all.

Q. But yet in our nature there are many spots?
A. Christ's blood therefore does perpetually wash them away.

Q. The memory and token of our sins may make us afraid?
A. All punishments due for them were taken away by the suffering of Christ.

Q. But yet we find sin working in us?
A. The death of Christ does kill the tyranny of it.

Q. Does it always remain in us to the end?
A. Yet through faith it is not imputed to the members of Christ.

Q. Why was he buried?
A. To assure us the better of his death.

Q. What does his burial teach us?
A. Continual mortification of sin.

Q. Why did he rise before us?
A. To assure us of his victory over death for us.

Q. What fruit do we get by his victory?
A. Hereby we are brought in a sure hope of life eternal. It works newness of life in us here. And it shall raise up our bodies again in the latter day.

Q. Why did he ascend into heaven before us?
A. To take possession of our inheritance in our name.

Q. But he said, "I shall be with you to the end?"
A. He spoke that of his spiritual presence.

Q. What does he do for us there now?
A. He makes continual intercession for us.

Q. What kind of intercession is it?
A. It is the continual mitigation of his Father's wrath for us through the virtue of his death.

Q. Is he our only intercessor and Mediator?
A. No doubt, seeing he only died for us.

Q. What does his sitting at the right hand mean?
A. The power he has in heaven and earth.

Q. What comfort do we have by his power and authority?
A. That we are in safely under his protection.

Q. For what cause will he come again?
A. To put a final end to our redemption.

Q. What shall be that end?
A. Eternal joy or misery to every man.

Q. Is not that done in every man's death?
A. No, for the bodies remain yet unrewarded.

Q. Shall there not be a middle state of men?
A. No, but all shall be brought to these two ends.

Q. Why will that be, seeing some are better and some are worse?
A. All shall be judged evil who are not members of Christ.

Q. But how can the quick be judged before they die?
A. Their sudden change shall be instead of death unto them.

Q. But all flesh should go to the dust again?
A. Ordinarily it is done so but here is a special cause.

Q. What comfort do we have of the person of the Judge?
A. Our Savior, Advocate, and Mediator, shall only be our Judge.

Q. What should the meditation of this article work in us?
A. The contempt of all other pleasures and a delight in heavenly things.

Q. Who shall be saved in that day?
A. All that are made here the members of the church.

Q. Who makes us members of Christ?
A. God's Holy Spirit only working in our hearts.

The third part of our belief

Q. What is the Holy Spirit?
A. He is God, equal with the Father and the Son.

Q. From where does he proceed?
A. From the Father and the Son.

Q. What is his office in general?
A. He puts all things in execution which are decreed by God's secret counsel.

Q. What does he do in the order of nature?
A. He keeps all things in their natural estate.

Q. Where do all of these alterations come from?
A. From the same Spirit working diversely in nature.

Q. Is the Spirit but nature then?
A. No for he is God ruling and keeping nature.

Q. What does he do in the worldly kingdoms?
A. He does raise and cast them down at his pleasure.

Q. Why are things attributed unto him?
A. Because he is the power and hand of God.

Q. What does he do in the kingdom of Christ?
A. He gathers all God's elect to Christ.

Q. Why is he called holy?
A. Because he is the fountain of holiness and makes us holy.

Q. When and how does he do this?
A. When by his mighty power he separated us from our natural corruption and dedicated us to godliness.

Q. What is this natural corruption?
A. A blindness of mind, hardness of heart, and contempt of God.

Q. How does he dedicate us to godliness?
A. He enlightens our minds, mollifies our hearts, and strengthens us.

Q. What then is all flesh without the Spirit of God?
A. Blind and dead in all heavenly things.

Q. What other names does he have in the Scriptures?
A. He is called the Spirit of faith, regeneration, strength, and comfort.

Q. Why are these names given to the Holy Spirit?
A. Because he works all these things in us.

Q. What are these graces called?
A. Sanctification, regeneration, or new birth and Spirit.

Q. What is our corrupted estate called?
A. The old man, old Adam, flesh and blood.

Q. What follows upon our sanctification?
A. A continual battle between the spirit and the flesh.

Q. Who strengthens and keeps us in the battle?
A. The same Spirit who also gives victory in the end.

Q. What is this battle to us?
A. A sure seal of the presence of the Holy Spirit.

Q. What battle has the old man in himself?
A. None at all against sin and wickedness.

Q. In whom then is this battle?
A. Only in the members of Christ and his church through the presence of the Spirit.

The fourth part of our belief

Q. What is the church which we confess here?
A. The whole company of God's elect called and sanctified.

Q. Do we believe in his church?
A. No, but we believe only in our God.

Q. What, then, do we believe about this Church?
A. That it was, is, and shall be to the end of the world.

Q. Why do we need to believe this?
A. For our great comfort and the glory of God.

Q. Explain that plainly?
A. The love of the Father, the death of Christ, and the power of the Spirit shall ever work in some.

Q. What follows this?
A. The glory of God and confusion of Satan with our comfort.

Q. Why is the Church only known to us by faith?
A. Because it contains only God's elect which are only known to him.

Q. When and how can we know them?
A. When we see the fruits of election and holiness in them.

Q. In what respect is the church called holy?
A. In respect of our justification and sanctification.

Q. How are these two graces different?
A. The first is perfect and the second imperfect.

Q. What is the reason for that diversity?
A. The first is in Christ and the second in us.

Q. Are not both of these gifts ours?
A. Yes no doubt seeing that Christ is ours.

Q. May we not come to a full perfection in this life?
A. No, for the flesh rebels continually against the Spirit.

Q. Why does the Spirit not sanctify us perfectly?
A. Least we should forget our former captivity and redemption?

Q. What admonition do we have of our estate?
A. We should be humble, repent, and be thankful to our God.

Q. Why is the church called universal?
A. Because it is spread throughout the whole world.

Q. How many churches are there in the world?
A. One church, one Christ: as one body and the head.

Q. Is it bound to any particular time, place, or persons?
A. No, for then it should not be universal.

Q. What is the communion of saints?
A. The mutual participation of Christ and his graces among his members.

Q. What follows upon this communion?
A. A spiritual uniting and communion among all Christ's members.

Q. Where is this communion grounded?
A. Upon their union with Christ their head.

Q. Who makes our union with Christ and among themselves?
A. The Holy Spirit by his mighty power.

Q. Is there any salvation without this communion?
A. None at all for Christ is the ground of salvation.

Q. May men be joined with Christ and not with all his saints?
A. No, nor yet with the saints if not with Christ.

Q. What then should our principal care be?
A. To hold fast our union with Christ our head.

Q. What follows upon that?
A. Then of necessity we are joined with all his saints and church.

Q. Should we not seek them and join with them externally also?
A. No doubt, whenever we see them or hear of them in particular.

How the church may be known

Q. How may we know this company externally?
A. By the true profession of the Word and holy sacraments.

Q. What if these marks are not found among them?
A. Then they are not the communion of saints.

Q. May we with safe conscience join ourselves with such?
A. No, for they are not the holy church of God where these marks are not.

Q. Then we depart from the universal Church.
A. No, but we depart from the corruption of men and remain in the holy universal church.

Q. But yet they will call themselves the church.
A. We should look to the true marks of the Church.

Q. May we leave the particular church where the Word is retained?
A. No, albeit various other vices abound there.

Q. But the multitudes are wicked and profane?
A. Yet there is a true church where the Word truly remains.

Q. What then is the infallible mark of Christ's church?
A. The Word truly preached and professed.

Q. Should we discuss who are and who are not indeed saints?
A. No, for that appertains to God only and to themselves.

Q. But by this way we are joined with the wicked in the body?
A. That cannot hurt us nor profit them.

Q. Why is that?
A. Because we and they are spiritually separated.

Q. But they make the word and the sacraments unfruitful.
A. Not to us but to themselves only.

Q. Why is remission of sins put here?
A. Because it is proper to the church and members of the same.

Q. Why is it proper for the church only?
A. Because only in the church is the Spirit of faith and repentance.

Q. Who forgives sins, by whom, and where?
A. Only God, through Christ, and his church here.

Q. How often are our sins forgiven?
A. Continually even until our lives end.

Q. What need is there for this?
A. Because sin is never thoroughly abolished here.

Q. How do we get remission of our sins?
A. Through the mercy of God and the merit of Christ.

Q. Is there any remission of sins after this life?
A. None at all, though some have taught otherwise.

Q. Is the sin and the pain both forgiven?
A. Yes, no doubt, seeing the one follows upon the other.

Q. But sometimes the pain remains after the sin?
A. The pain is not a satisfaction for sin.

Q. What is it, then, seeing it comes of sin?
A. It is a Fatherly correction and medicine preservative.

Q. What are we to yet look for at the hand of our God?
A. The resurrection of our bodies and eternal life.

Q. With what bodies shall we rise again?
A. With the same bodies in substance as Christ did rise.

Q. But the apostle says that our bodies shall be spiritual?
A. That is in respect of their present estate.

Q. Of what condition shall our bodies be then?
A. Free from all corruption and alteration.

Q. Why will we rise with the same bodies?
A. That they may receive their reward with the souls.

Q. What admonition do we have given to us here?
A. That we should dedicate our bodies to the service of God.

Q. But the wicked will be partakers of the same resurrection?
A. No doubt, but to their great confusion.

Q. Many doubt this resurrection?
A. But we are sure that he which fulfilled the first promises, can and will perform the rest.

Q. What kind of life is promised to us?
A. Eternal life without any misery.

Q. What is prepared for the wicked?
A. Eternal death without any joy.

Q. Yet they shall live eternally?
A. That life shall be to live in eternal death.

Q. What admonition do we have here?
A. That we should wait continually for the coming of the Lord.

Q. What other admonition do we have here?
A. We should thirst continually for eternal life.

Q. Is it enough to know these things to be true?
A. No, but we must know and apply them to ourselves.

Q. What are these articles which we have declared?
A. The ground and foundation of our faith and religion.

Q. How should we apply them to ourselves?
A. By our own true and lively faith.

Of true faith with the fruits

Q. What is true faith?
A. An assured knowledge of God's mercy toward us for Christ's sake according to his promise.

Q. Do we have any natural inclination to this faith?
A. None at all, but rather a natural rebellion.

Q. Who then works these things in us?
A. God's Holy Spirit seals them in our hearts.

Q. How can guilty men be assured of God's mercy.
A. By the truth of his promise made to the penitent.

Q. Yet our guiltiness cannot but fear God's justice?
A. Therefore we set between us and it the satisfaction of Christ.

The first fruit of faith

Q. What is the first fruit of faith?
A. By it we are made one with Christ our head.

Q. How is the union made and when?
A. When we are made flesh of his flesh and bone of his bones.

Q. Was not this done when he took our flesh?
A. No, for he only then was made flesh of our flesh.

Q. When are we made flesh of his flesh?
A. When we are united with him spiritually as lively members with the head.

The second fruit of faith

Q. What do we get by this union?
A. We are made partakers of all his graces and merits and our sins are imputed to him and abolished from us.

Q. What chiefly follows?
A. A perfect justification and peace of conscience.

Q. Where does our justification stand?
A. In remission of sins and imputation of justice.

Q. How can God's justice forgive sin without satisfaction?
A. Christ satisfied abundantly the justice of God for us.

Q. Whole justice is imputed to us?
A. The perfect obedience and justice of Christ.

Q. How can another man's justice be made ours?
A. Christ is not another man to us properly.

Q. Why is he not another man to us?
A. Because he is given to us freely of the Father with all his graces and we are joined with him.

Q. How is justification offered to us?
A. By the preaching of the gospel.

Q. How do we receive justification?
A. Only by our own lively faith.

Q. Is not justification offered to us by the Law?
A. Yes, but no man is able to fulfill the Law.

Q. What if a man lives godly and uprightly?
A. No upright living can be without faith.

Q. Is our faith perfect in all points?
A. No, for it is joined with manifold imperfections.

Q. How then can it justify us?
A. It is only the instrument of our justification.

Q. What justifies us properly?
A. Only Jesus Christ by his perfect justice.

The third fruit of faith

Q. Can our faith be without a godly life?
A. No more than fire without heat.

Q. What is the reason for that?
A. Because Christ sanctifies all whom he justifies.

Q. Do the good works of the faithful not merit eternal life?
A. No, for then Christ should not only be our Savior.

Q. Yet the good works of the faithful please God?
A. Yes no doubt, but yet through faith only do they please him.

Q. Why do they not please God seeing they are the works of the Spirit?
A. Because they are defiled with the infirmities of the flesh.

Q. Are our good works unprofitable then?
A. That does not follow seeing they please God and have rewards both here and there.

Q. Does the gospel teach us to condemn good works?
A. No, for it requires continual faith and repentance.

Of Repentance

Q. What is true repentance?
A. It is the hatred of sin and love of justice.

Q. From where does this proceed?
A. From the fear of God and hope of mercy.

Q. How are we brought to this fear of God?
A. Through the preaching of the Law.

Q. How do we come to the hope of mercy?
A. By the preaching of the gospel.

Q. What does repentance work in us?
A. Continual mortification of our lusts and newness of life.

Q. Who works these two things in us?
A. The Spirit of regeneration through the death and resurrection of Christ.

Q. How long should we continue in repentance?
A. All the days of our lives.

Q. What is this exercise before God?
A. His spiritual service and our chief obedience.

Q. What is the rule of Christian repentance?
A. God's holy Law, which is the rule of all godliness of life.

5.

THE SECOND PART OF GOD'S HONOR IS OBEDIENCE. HERE THE LAW IS DECLARED AND HOW IT DOES DIFFER FROM THE GOSPEL

Q. Recite the words of the Law (Exodus 20).
A. Then God spoke all these words saying, "I am the LORD your God, who brought you out of the land of Egypt, out of the house of slavery.

1. You shall have no other gods before Me.
2. You shall not make for yourself an idol, or any likeness of what is in heaven above or on the earth beeneath or in the water under the earth. You shall not worship them or serve them; for I, the LORD your God, am a jealous God, visiting the iniquity of the fathers on the children, on the third

and the fourth generations of those who hate Me, but showing lovingkindness to thousands, to those who love Me and keep My commandments.

3. You shall not take the name of the LORD your God in vain, for the LORD will not leave him unpunished who takes His name in vain.
4. Remember the sabbath day, to keep it holy. [9] Six days you shall labor and do all your work, [10] but the seventh day is a sabbath of the LORD your God; *in it* you shall not do any work, you or your son or your daughter, your male or your female servant or your cattle or your sojourner who stays with you. [11] For in six days the LORD made the heavens and the earth, the sea and all that is in them, and rested on the seventh day; therefore the LORD blessed the sabbath day and made it holy.
5. Honor your father and your mother, that your days may be prolonged in the land which the LORD your God gives you.
6. You shall not murder.
7. You shall not commit adultery.
8. You shall not steal.
9. You shall not bear false witness against your neighbor.
10. You shall not covet your neighbor's house; you shall not covet your neighbor's wife or his male servant or his female servant or his ox or his donkey or anything that belongs to your neighbor.

Q. Who gave this law first to Moses?
A. The eternal God, distinct in two Tables.

Q. What does this law teach?
A. It teaches and requires our duty toward God and man.

Q. Is the Law perfect in all points?
A. Yes no doubt, seeing it came from the fountain of all perfection.

Q. Does the Law only require external obedience?
A. No, but it requires all the purity of the spirit.

Q. What reward and pain does the Law propound?
A. The blessing of God to the keepers of this law and his curse to the breakers thereof.

Q. How many commandements are in the first table?
A. Four, which declare our duty to our God.

Q. How many are in the second table?
A. Six, which declare our duty to our neighbour.

Q. What is contained in every commandment?
A. One thing is commanded and the contrary forbidden.

Q. What does the preface of the Law contain?
A. The reasons why God should command and we obey.

Q. What are these reasons?
A. His Majesty, power, promise, benefits, our promise to him.

1. You shall have no other God's, etc.

Q. What is forbidden in this first commandement?
A. All forging or worshipping of false gods.

Q. What is a false god?
A. Everything we place in God's place.

Q. When do we place anything in God's place?
A. When we give it God's due honor.

Q. What is God's due honor?
A. Faith, fear, prayer, thanks, and obedience.

Q. What is commanded here?
A. That we settle ourselves upon the one and only true God.

Q. Why is this commandement put here first?
A. Because it is the ground of all the rest.

Q. Why does he say, "before my face?"
A. Because he requires the purity of the heart.

2. You shall make for yourself no idol, etc.

Q. What is forbidden in the second commandment?
A. That we neither represent nor worship God by any image.

Q. Is every kind of imagery forbidden here?
A. No, but only that in which God is represented or honored.

Q. What is forbidden in general here?
A. All corrupting of God's service by the inventions of men.

Q. What is required here?
A. That we worship God according to his Word.

Q. What kind of service does he require of us?
A. Both inward and outward service.

Q. Can we not serve him externally as we please?
A. No, for that kind of service is cursed idolatry.

Q. Does God condemn the external service?
A. Yes, if it has not the inward service.

Q. What is it called without the inward service?
A. The dead or dumb letter.

Q. What is the other service called?
A. The Spirit, which gives life to all external service commanded by God.

Q. Why is this commandment put in the second place?
A. Because it declares how the true God should be served?

Q. Why is the promise and the threatening added?
A. To move us more willingly to give obedience.

Q. Why is the promise longer than the threatening?
A. Because he is more ready to give mercy than to give judgment.

3. You shall not take the name, etc.

Q. What is forbidden in this third commandment?
A. All dishonoring and abuse of God's majesty.

Q. What is commanded here?
A. All kind of honor and reverence due to his majesty.

Q. What is meant here by his name?
A. All the titles and names representing his majesty.

Q. What represents him?
A. His word, sacraments, and works.

Q. How should we honor his name?
A. With heart, mouth, and deed to our power.

Q. When is this done?
A. When we think, speak, and work all things to his glory.

Q. May we swear by his name?
A. We may and should for good causes.

Q. What does the added threat mean?
A. The great regard he has to his own honor.

4. Remember the Sabbath, to keep it holy, etc.

Q. What does this fourth commandment require?
A. That we keep the Sabbath holy to the Lord.

Q. When and how is this done?
A. When we bestow it only in God's service.

Q. Why is God's example added?
A. To move us more earnestly to follow him.

Q. Is there any holiness in that day above the rest?
A. No for the holiness is only in the exercise.

Q. What if the exercise is not kept?
A. Then it is made the devil's own feast day.

Q. May we work upon all other days?
A. Yes for God has given us free liberty.

Q. Why was there one day appointed?
A. To maintain the true religion in the church.

Q. For what other cause was it given?
A. For the ease of servants and beasts.

Q. Was it to the Jews a sacrament of their spiritual rest?
A. Yes, but that ceremony is taken away by Christ.

Q. Why was it taken away?
A. Because we have spritual rest by him.

5. Honor your father and mother, etc.

Q. What does this fifth commandment require?
A. That we honor all such as God has placed above us.

Q. Who are those persons?
A. Parents, pastors, magistrates, husbands, and masters.

Q. What honor should we give them?
A. Love, fear, obedidence, and help in their need.

Q. What equity has this commandment?
A. This, because these persons are placed in God's place for our comfort.

Q. How far should we obey them?
A. So far as the Word of God commands.

Q. What if they command anything against the Word?
A. Then we must obey God rather than men.

Q. What does the added promise contain?
A. It contains the contrary threatening for the breakers.

Q. But neither of them is absolutely kept?
A. Therefore the blessing and the curse remains always sure.

Q. Why is this promise and threatening in special added?
A. Because these superiors are preservers of our lives and livings.

6. You shall not kill

Q. What is forbidden in this sixth commandment?
A. All envy, rancor, and hatred with the fruits.

Q. What is commanded here?
A. Brotherly love with the fruits and signs?

Q. What is the final end of this commandment?
A. The preservation of our neighbor's life.

7. You shall not commit adultery

Q. What is forbidden in the seventh commandment?
A. All filthy lusts in our heart, word, or deed, or signs.

Q. What is commanded here?
A. All kind of chastity and means to keep it.

Q. Is marriage condemned here?
A. No, but rather hereby it is established.

Q. What is the end of this commandment?
A. That we keep both our bodies and hearts pure and clean.

8. You shall not steal

Q. What is forbidden in the eighth commandment?
A. All wrong and deceitful dealing with our neighbor.

Q. What is commanded here?
A. Equity and justice to every man.

Q. How should this be done?
A. With mind, heart, mouth, and deed to our power.

Q. What is the end of this commandment?
A. That we labor so that every man have his own.

9. You shall not bear false witness, etc.

Q. What is forbidden in the ninth commandment?
A.False reports of our neighbor and hearing of them.

Q. Is this enough for our discharge?
A. No, for the uprightness of the heart is required also.

Q. What is the end of this commandment?
A. That the simple truth ever be among us.

10. You shall not covet, etc.

Q. What is forbidden in this last commandment?
A. All light and sudden motions to evil.

Q. Were not those motions forbidden before?
A. No, but the consent and deed were only forbidden.

Q. Then what degrees of sins are forbidden?
A. The lust, the consent, and the deed.

Q. What is this lust?
A. Original infection and mother of the rest of our sins.

Q. What is commanded here?
A. The perfect love of our neighbor with the fruits.

Q. Who is our neighbour?
A. Every man, friend or foe.

Q. What is the reason for this Law?
A. In that we are all brethren and bear the image of our God.

The summary of the Law

Q. What is the sum and end of these commandments?
A. The perfect love of God and our neighbor.

Q. When is our love perfect and the law absolutely fulfilled?
A. When all parts of our minds and hearts are replenished with the love of God and our neighbor.

Q. Has anyone ever fulfilled this law?
A. None at all, except Jesus Christ.

Q. What do they get, then, who seek salvation by the Law?
A. Their own double condemnation.

Q. Why did God give this straight Law to mankind?
A. Because it agrees with his nature and our first estate.

Q. But we are changed and made weak through sin.
A. Yet God has not changed his will and Law.

Q. Is all flesh hereby accursed and damned?
A. Yes, but God has given a sufficient remedy in Christ.

Q. Declare how that is, seeing the Law does curse?
A. By faith we escape the curse and get the blessing of the Law.

The use of the law

Q. To what purpose then does the Law serve?
A. It is profitable both to the faithful and unfaithful.

Q. What profit does it bring to the unfaithful?
A. It shows their sin and just condemnation.

Q. But that is rather hurtful to them?
A. No, for by it they are sent to Christ.

Q. But many others despair or become worse?
A. That does not come from the Law but from our corrupt nature.

Q. When are they sent to Christ by the Law?
A. When they get a taste of mercy in Christ after that they are humbled by the Law.

Q. Is this the ordinary way of our conversion?
A. Yes no doubt for Christ saves only the humbled.

Q. What profit do the faithful gain by the Law?
A. It puts them daily in remembrance of their sins.

Q. What good fruit comes from that?
A. Humility and an earnest dependence upon Christ.

Q. What other profit do they have by the Law?
A. It is a bridle to their affections and a rule of all godliness.

Q. If it is a bridle do they not then hate the Law?
A. No, they hate their own affections and love the Law.

Q. Does this knowledge come by the Law?
A. No, but by the knowledge of the gospel.

The difference between the Law and the gospel

Q. From where does this difference come from?
A. From the Spirit which is joined with the gospel and not with the Law.

Q. What follows upon this?
A. The Law commands but it gives no strength.

Q. What does the gospel do?
A. It freely gives all that it requires of us.

Q. What other differences are there between them?
A. The Law has no compassion upon sinners.

Q. What about the gospel?
A. It offers mercy only to sinners.

Q. What other difference are there?
A. In the manner of our justification.

Q. What does the Law require in our justification?
A. Our own perfect obedience.

Q. What does the gospel require?
A. Only faith in the obedience of Christ Jesus.

Q. Does the gospel favor the transgression of the Law?
A. No, but it gives strength to obey the Law.

How the Law and the Gospel agree.

Q. Where do the Law and the gospel agree?
A. They are both from God and declare one kind of justice.

Q. What is that one kind of justice?
A. The perfect love of God and our neighbor.

Q. What follows from this?
A. That the severe Law pronounces all the faithful just.

Q. How can the Law pronounce them just?
A. Because they have in Christ all that the Law requires.

Q. But yet they remain transgressors of the Law?
A. That is in themselves and yet are just in Christ and in themselves love justice.

Q. What then is the estate of the faithful here?
A. They are sure in Christ and yet fighting against sin.

Q. What battle do we have?
A. We battle both within and without.

Q. What battle do we have within?
A. The battle of the flesh against the Spirit.

Q. What battle do we have without?
A. The temptations of Satan and the world.

Q. What armor do we have?
A. True faith with fervent prayer to our God.

Q. Is prayer the cause of our victory?
A. No, but it is a means by which God does save us and he is honored by it.

6.
THE THIRD PART OF GOD'S HONOR IS PRAYER, WHICH IS DECLARED IN GENERAL, WITH AN EXPOSITION OF THE LORD'S PRAYER

Q. What is prayer or calling upon God?
A. It is a humble lifting up of our minds and hearts to God.

Q. Why do we go only to God in our prayers?
A. Because prayer is part of his true worshipping.

Q. Why then do we seek needful things from men?
A. Because they are appointed stewards to us.

Q. How should we go to them?
A. As to God's instruments only.

Q. To whom should we give praise?
A. Only to God to whom all praise belongs.

Q. Can we pray to saints and angels?
A. No, for that is manifest idolatry.

Q. And are the angels appointed to serve us?
A. Yes, but we have no commandement to seek from them.

Q. What shall we say of the common custom used in the time of blindness?
A. We should be content with the order appointed by God.

Q. How should we pray to our God?
A. With our minds and hearts for he is a Spirit.

Q. What is a prayer without the mind and heart?
A. It is unprofitable and cursed of God.

Q. What manner of mind and affection is required?
A. First an earnest feeling of our own misery through sin.

Q. What is required next?
A. A fervent desire with faith and hope to obtain.

Q. Who moves us to pray fervently?
A. Only God's Holy Spirit.

Q. Should this make us cold in prayer?
A. No, but rather fervent in calling on the Spirit.

Q. What is the value of prayer with the tongue?
A. It profits much if the mind be with it.

Q. What is prayer in a strange language?
A. It is a plain mockery of God.

Q. Should we be sure to be heard in our prayer?
A. Otherwise we pray in vain and without faith.

Q. What are the grounds of our assurance?
A. God's promise, his Spirit in us, and our Mediator.

Q. In whose name should we pray?
A. In the name of our Lord Jesus Christ.

Q. How can that be proven?
A. By God's commandement and promise to hear us in so doing.

Q. What thing should we ask of God?
A. All things promised or commanded in the Word.

Q. Can we not follow our own fantasy in our prayer?
A. No, for then our prayer should be very vain.

Q. Why is that, since all men desire good things?
A. Because we neither know nor desire the things that are best for us.

Q. What then should we do in our prayers?
A. We must learn of God, what, and how we should ask.

Q. How then should we begin our prayer?
A. We should first submit our affections to God's will.

Q. What rule has God given us for this purpose?
A. The Scriptures and chiefly the Lord's Prayer.

Q. Recite the Lord's Prayer? (Matthew 6:9ff.)
A. Our Father who is in heaven.

1. Hallowed be Your name. Your kingdome come. Your will be done, On earth as it is in heaven.
2. Give us this day our daily bread. And forgive us our debts, as we also have forgiven our debtors. And do not lead us into temptation, but deliver us from evil. For Yours is the kingdom and the power and the glory forever. Amen.

The divions and order of prayer

Q. How is this prayer divided?
A. Into a preface and six petitions.

Q. How do the six petitions differ?
A. The first three appertain only to the glory of God.

Q. What do the other three appertain?
A. To our comfort principally.

Q. What should we seek first in our prayer?
A. The glory of our God before all things.

Q. Is that not hard to flesh and blood?
A. Yes, but it is only the work of God's Holy Spirit.

Q. Are we not happy when God is glorified in us?
A. Yes no doubt, but we should look only to God's glory.

Q. Do not the other three tend to the same end?
A. Yes, but we are permitted to look to ourselves also.

Q. For what use does the preface serve?
A. To prepare ourselves to pray aright.

The Preface

Q. Why do we call him Father?
A. To assure us of his good will.

Q. Why do we call him our Father in common?
A. Because our prayers should be for our brethren also.

Q. What is meant here by the heaven?
A. God's majesty, power, and glory.

Q. What purpose do these things serve in our prayer?
A. By them we are prepared for reverence and hope.

The first part

Q. What thing is meant here by his name?
A. His due honor, glory, fame, and estimation.

Q. Can his honor either increase or diminish?
A. Not in itself but only in the hearts of men.

Q. What thing do we desire here first?
A. Our Father's honor and glory in this world.

Q. When and how is this done?
A. When with heart, mouth, and deed, he is extolled above all things.

Q. How are men brought to do this?
A. By the lively knowledge of his majesty.

Q. How can his unsearchable majesty be known?
A. By his word, sacraments, and manifold works.

Q. What should men learn by these names?
A. His infinite power, goodness, mercy, justice, providence, truth and constancy, etc.

Q. Is it not enough that we ourselves honor his name?
A. No, but we should desire and labor that the same be done in all men according to our power and vocation.

Q. When and where should we do this?
A. In propserity and adversity, privately, and publicly.

Q. What if we find fault with his Word or works?
A. Then we extol our name and profane his holy name.

Q. What if we be nothing moved at the profaning of his name?
A. Then we are not the sons of God.

Q. From where does this petition flow?
A. From a vehement affection to our Father's glory.

Q. What is this affection to us?
A. A plain testimony of our adoption.

Q. What is our desire when we pray for his kingdom?
A. That he might reign more and more in the hearts of his chosen.

Q. When is this thing done?
A. When the Spirit reforms and rules our hearts.

Q. What other things do we ask here?
A. That the tyranny of Satan be beaten down.

Q. What purpose does the third petition serve?
A. Through it the other two are performd.

Q Explain that more plainely?
A. His name is sanctified and he reigns when his will is done.

Q. Are not all things compelled to obey his will?
A. Yes, but we speak here of men's voluntary obedience.

Q. How can that be proven?
A. By the comparison added here.

Q. When shall these three petitions be performed perfectly?
A. Never in this world by reason of our corruption.

Q. Why should we pray for things that will not be?
A. We always desire what ought to be and one day shall be done.

Q. But all those things shall come to pass whether we pray or not?
A. No doubt, yet herein we declare our good will to our Father's glory.

Q. What should we gather of this?
A. This, that he is not the child of God that seeks not this before all things.

Q. Do we not pray here against our own natural wills?
A. Yes no doubt, for we desire them to be reformd according to God's will.

The second part

Q. What do we mean by our daily bread?
A. All things needful for this present life.

Q. But he commands us to labor for it?
A. Our labors are vain without his blessing.

Q. Why do we call it ours seeing it is his gift?
A. Because we ask no more than is given us by lawful means.

Q. Why do we only ask for this day?
A. To teach us to be content with his present provision.

Q. Then must we beg daily at his hand?
A. Our joy stands to daily depend on him.

Q. Do the rich have need of this daily seeking?
A. Yes, no doubt for riches have not always the blessing of God.

Q. What are we to ask in the other two petitions?
A. The continual comfort of our souls.

Q. Why should we seek the comfort of our bodies first?
A. To assure us the better of our spiritual comfort.

Q. Explain that.
A. If he takes care of our bodies how much more shall he provide for our souls.

Q. What are we to seek in this fifth petition?
A. The remission of our sins or spiritual debts.

Q. Why are our sins called debts?
A. Because they bind us to an everlasting pain.

Q. Why do we desire free remission?
A. Because by no means can we satisfy them.

Q. Is the pain remitted freely with the sin?
A. Yes, for Christ satisfied fully for us.

Q. Should every man pray thus continually?
A. Yes, for all flesh is subject to sin.

Q. But sometimes men do good things.
A. Yet they sin in the best things they do.

Q. What profit do we get by this petition?
A. Only in this way, both we and our works please God.

Q. Why is the condition added?
A. To put us in remembrance of our duty.

Q. What is our duty?
A. To forgive freely all offenses done to us.

Q. Is this the reason why we seek remission?
A. No, but we allege it for a mark that we bear the inward scale of God's children.

Q. What is that inward scale of God's children?
A. The image of God who does freely forgive.

Q. What does this image work in all his children?
A. Free remission of all offenses done to them.

Q. What are they that will not forgive?
A. Those that bear not the image of our heavenly Father.

Q. What are we asking in the last petition?
A. Defense against all temptations to evil.

Q. Does every man need this defense?
A. Yes, no doubt for without it no flesh can stand.

Q. Why since we have the Spirit?
A. Because the dangers are great and many within and without us.

Q. By what way are we preserved from these temptations?
A. By the mighty power of the Spirit working in us.

Q. Does God draw any man to wickedness?
A. No, for that is contrary to his nature.

Q. Why then, do we ask God this?
A. Because no man is led in sin without his willing permission.

Q. Who does lead men properly to sin?
A. Satan and men's own wicked lusts.

Q. When does God willingly permit men to be led?
A. When he delivered them to Satan and their own lusts.

Q. What moves our good God to do this to men?
A. His justice provoked through their ingratitude.

Q. What does Satan mean in leading men from sin to sin?
A. Malice conceived both against God and man.

Q. Do all kind of temptations proceed from Satan?
A. No, for God often tempts men also.

Q. When and how does he do this?
A. When he offers occasions to discover their hearts.

Q. What things are discovered then?
A. Notable gifts of his or monstrous sins of theirs.

Q. Should we desire that we thus be tried?
A. No, for that would not be profitable for us.

Q. What should we gather of these last petitions?
A. That we commit both body and soul to God's providence.

Q. What else should we observe?
A. That we pray for the welfare of our brethren.

Q. May we not change the form of this prayer?
A. We may change the words but not the sense.

Q. But every man may pray particularly for himself?
A. Yet he may not exclude the welfare of his brethren.

Q. Are all things needful for us contained in this prayer?
A. Yes, seeing the wisdom of God gave it.

Q. What time chiefly should we use prayer?
A. At all times but principally in time of trouble.

Q. What if God delay to grant our petitions?
A. We should continue in prayer with patience and hope.

Q. What should we hope of his long delay?
A. That he will turn all thinges to our comfort.

Q. What does the clause, "For thine is the kingdom," etc. added here mean?
A. It declares the cause and ground of our prayer to God.

Q. What else are we taught here?
A. That we should conclude our prayers with thanksgiving.

7.
THE FOURTH PART OF GOD'S HONOR IS THANKSGIVING, WHERE THE CAUSES, THE RULE, AND OTHER CIRCUMSTANCES OF THANKS ARE DECLARED

Q. What is thanksgiving or praising of God?
A. It is to acknowledge him to be the author and fountain of all good things.

Q. Can we not give thanks to angels or saints?
A. No, for that would manifest idolatry.

Q. Should we not be thankful to men?
A. Yes, but the chief praise pertains to God.

Q. How should we praise him?
A. With mind, heart, mouth, and works.

Q. What rules of thanksgiving do we have?
A. The Scripture and examples of his servants.

Q. For what cause should we praise him?
A. For his infinite benefits, corporal and spiritual.

Q. But we are oftentimes in great misery?
A. Yet for that also we should praise him.

Q. Why is that?
A. Because he turns all things to our comfort.

Q. By whom should we praise him?
A. Only by Jesus Christ.

Q. Why only him?
A. Because only through Christ we receive his graces.

Q. Where should we praise God?
A. Both publicly and privately.

Q. How long should we praise him?
A. So long as we enioy his benefits.

Q. How do prayer and thanksgiving differ?
A. Prayer seeks and thanksgiving grants our prayer heard or delayed for our comfort.

Q. What other differences are there?
A. Prayer in a part may cease for a time but not thanksgiving

Q. What is the cause of that?
A. Because we have always some benefits of God.

Q. How should we then begin and end our prayer?
A. Evermore with thanksgiving to our God.

Q. Did the Fathers have a sacrifice of praise?
A. Yes, and all that we do in faith is a sacrifice of thanks.

Q. What can we gather of all that we have spoken?
A. That this is life eternal: to know God through Jesus Christ and to honor him rightly.

Q. What are these four parts of God's honor?
A. They are only his service pleasing him.

Q. What are these four parts to us?
A. Infallible seals of our election and salvation.

Q. By whom are we kept in this estate?
A. By the power of the Holy Spirit.

Q. What instruments does he use for this purpose?
A. The Word, the sacraments, and ministry of men.

8.
THE ORDINARY INSTRUMENTS TO SALVATION ARE THESE: THE WORD, THE SACRAMENTS, AND MINISTRY OF MEN WHICH ARE PARTICULARLY DECLARED.

Of the Word of God

Q. How should we behave ourselves toward the Word?
A. We should love, receive, and obey it as God's eternal truth.

Q. But it comes to us only by men?
A. Yet always we should receive it as sent of God.

Q. Who can assure us of this?
A. Only the Holy Spirit working in our hearts.

Q. How should we use the Word?
A. We should read it and hear it reverently.

Q. May common people read the Scriptures?
A. They may and are commanded to read them.

Q. May they have them in their own language?
A. Without a doubt for otherwise they could not profit.

Q. Is not private reading sufficient for us?
A. No, if public teaching may be had.

Q. How can that be proven?
A. Thus, as the ministers are commanded to teach, even so are we commanded to hear them.

Q. How far should we obey their doctrine?
A. So far as it agrees with the Word.

Q. How long should we continue to hear?
A. As long as we live and teaching may be had.

Q. What need is there of this continual hearing?
A. Because we are both ignorant and forgetful.

Q. What shall we judge of them that will not hear?
A. They refuse the helping hand of God.

Q. What shall we do when preaching cannot be had?
A. We should read Scripture with all diligence.

Q. What if we cannot read them?
A. We should have recourse to them which can read.

Q. Are the Scriptures obscure and hard?
A. The Holy Spirit will help the willing.

Q. What if we were once well instructed by our pastors?
A. Yet we must continue in this school to the end.

Q. Why is that if we are once sufficiently instructed?
A. God has established this order in his church because we need to be continually instructed.

Q. What follows this?
A. The ministers or pastors are needful for us.

Q. But they are commonly neglected and contemned?
A. Whosoever contemns them contemns God and his own salvation.

Q. What should this continual exercise work in us?
A. Increase of faith and godliness of life.

Q. What if these two things do not follow?
A. Then in vain is our reading and hearing.

Q. What else is joined with the Word for our comfort?
A. The holy sacraments of Jesus Christ.

Of the sacraments in general

Q. What is a sacrament?
A. A sensible sign and seal of God's favor offered and given to us.

Q. To what end are the sacraments given?
A. To nourish our faith in the promise of God.

Q. How can sensible signs do this?
A. They have this office of God and not of themselves.

Q. It is the only office of the Spirit to nourish our faith?
A. Yet they are added as effectual instruments of the Spirit.

Q. Where, then, does the efficacy of the sacraments come from?
A. Only from God's Holy Spirit.

Q. What moved God to use this kind of teaching?
A. Because it is natural to us to understand heavenly things by sensible and earthly things.

Q. Can we be saved without the sacraments?
A. Yes, for our salvation does not absolutely depend upon them.

Q. Can we refuse to use the sacraments?
A. No, for then we should refuse the favor of God.

Q. Do all men receive the favor of God by them?
A. No, but only the faithful receive it.

Q. How then are they true seals to all men?
A. They offer Christ truly to all men.

Q. When are the sacraments fruitful?
A. When we receive them with faith.

Q. Is there any virtue enclosed in them?
A. None at all, for they are but signs of heavenly mysteries.

Q. What should our faith seek by them?
A. To be led directly to Jesus Christ.

Q. If they require faith first how can they nourish faith?
A. They require some faith first and then they nourish the same.

Q. Are we not unbelievers when we need signs?
A. No, but rather we are weak in faith.

Q. What then is our estate in this life?
A. We are always imperfect and weak in faith.

Q. What then should we do?
A. We should diligently use the Word and the sacraments.

How the sacraments and the Word differ and agree

Q. How do the sacraments differ from the Word?
A. They speak to the eye and the Word to the ear.

Q. They speak other things than the Word?
A. No, but the same thing differently.

Q. But the Word does teach us sufficiently?
A. Yet the sacramentes with the Word do it more effectually.

Q. What then are the sacramentes to the Word?
A. They are sure and authentic seals given by God.

Q. Can the sacraments be without the Word?
A. No, for the Word is their life.

Q. Can the Word be fruitful without the sacraments?
A. Yes, no doubt but it works more plenteously with them.

Q. What is the cause of that?
A. Because more senses are moved to the comfort of our faith.

The parts of the sacraments

Q. What are the principal parts of the sacrament?
A. The external action and the inward signification.

Q. How are they joined together?
A. As the Word and the signification.

Q. What similitude have the sacramentes with the sign signified by them?
A. Great similitude in substance and in qualities.

Q. What signifies the substance of the elements?
A. The very substance of Christ's body.

Q. What if the substance of the elements were not there?
A. Then they were not true sacramentes of Christ's body.

Q. What do the natural qualities of the elements mean?
A. The spiritual qualities given by Christ.

Q. What does our near conjunction with the sacraments signify?
A. Our spiritual union with Jesus Christ and among ourselves.

Q. What does the outward giving and taking mean?
A. The spiritual giving or taking of Christ.

Q. What does the the natural operation of the elements mean?
A. The spiritual operation of Christ in us.

Q. Are these only signified by the sacraments?
A. No, but they are also given and sealed up by the Spirit.

Q. Who can give the seal of these things?
A. Only God can give the seal of his promise.

Of the minister and order of the sacraments

Q. Who can administer the sacraments?
A. Only the minister of the Word of God.

Q. In what manner should they be ministered?
A. According to the order given by Christ.

Q. How are they sanctified, consecrated, or blessed?
A. By the practice of the order commanded by Christ.

Q. What does it mean to consecrate or bless a sacrament?
A. It is to apply a common thing to a holy use.

Q. Who can do this?
A. Only God and only at his commandment.

Q. Does the consecration or blessing change the substance of the elements?
A. No, for it only changes the use.

Q. How long do they remain holy?
A. So long as they are used in that action.

Q. What are they after that use?
A. Common things as before.

Q. Do the sacramentes profit all the receivers when they are administred?
A. No, seeing they are received by some without faith for a time.

Q. Then the words of consecration have no force?
A. They have no force to imprint any quality in the elements of virtue or holines.

Q. To whom are they spoken?
A. To the receivers and to the elements.

Q. What is the office of those words of blessing?
A. To testify the will of God to the people.

Q. In what language should they be spoken?
A. In the receivers own language.

Q. Where should the sacraments be administred?
A. Publically before the congregation.

Of the Receivers

Q. To whom should the sacraments be given?
A. To all the members of the church in due time.

Q. How should the sacraments be received?
A. In a lively faith and true repentance.

Q. What if there is no faith and repentance?
A. Then double condemnation is sealed up.

Q. Can the sins of the ministers or others hurt us?
A. No, for they are God's ordinances.

Q. How should we prepare ourselves?
A. We should try our knowledge, faith, and repentance.

Q. Should these gifts be perfect in us?
A. Not so but they should be found and without hypocrisy.

The causes and number of the sacraments

Q. To what end are the sacraments used?
A. For the nourishment of our faith and for an open protestation of our religion before men.

Q. What other end do they serve?
A. They require the increase of newness of life with brotherly love and peace.

Q. Did the sacramentes of the Old Testament serve for the same uses?
A. Yes no doubt as the prophets and apostles do testify.

Q. How many sacraments has Christ given us?
A. Only two, baptism and the Lord's Supper.

Q. Why do we only have these two sacraments?
A. Because we need both to be received and also feed in God's family.

Q. Did not the Fathers have very many sacraments?
A. Yet they had but two principal ones, that is circumcision and the Passover.

Q. What did these two testify to them?
A. Their receiving and continual feeding in God's household.

Of the sacrament of baptism

Q. What is the significance of baptism?
A. Remission of our sins and regeneration.

Q. What resemblance has baptism with remission of sins?
A. As washing cleans the body so Christ's blood cleans our souls.

Q. Where does this cleansing stand?
A. In putting away of sin and imputation of justice.

Q. Where stands our regeneration?
A. In mortification and newness of life.

Q. How are these things sealed up in baptism?
A. By the laying on of water.

Q. What does the laying on of the water signify?
A. Our dying to sin and rising to righteousness.

Q. Does the external washing work these things?
A. No it is only the work of God's Holy Spirit.

Q. Then the sacrament is a bare figure?
A. No, but it has the reality joined with it.

Q. Do all men receive these graces with the sacraments?
A. No, but only the faithful.

Q. What is the ground of our regeneration?
A. The death, burial, and resurrection of Christ.

Q. When are we partakers of his death and resurrection?
A. When we are made one with him through his Spirit

Q. How should we rightly use baptism?
A. We should use it in faith and repentence.

Q. How long does baptism work?
A. All the days of our life.

Of the baptism of children

Q. How then may little children receive baptism?
A. Even as they received circumcision under the Law.

Q.Upon what ground were they circumcised?
A. Upon the ground made to the Fathers and their seed.

Q. Do we have the same promise for us and our children?
A. No doubt seeing Christ came to accomplish the same to the faithful.

Q. What if our children die without baptism?
A. Yet they are saved by the promise.

Q. Why are they baptized, see they are young and do not understand?
A. Because they are of the seed of the faithful.

Q. What comfort do we have by their baptism?
A. This, that we rest persuaded they are inheritors of the kingdom of heaven.

Q. What should that work in us?
A. Diligence to teach them the way of salvation.

Q. What admonition do they have hereby?
A. That they should be thankful when they come to age.

Q. What then is baptism to our children?
A. An entry into the church of God and to the holy supper.

Q. How does baptism differ from the Lord's Supper?
A. In the element, action, rites, and signification.

Q. Why is baptism administered only once?
A. Because it is enough to be once received into God's family.

Q. Why is the Lord's Supper administered so often?
A. Because we have need to be fed continually.

Q. Why is the Lord's Supper not ministered also to infants?
A. Because they cannot examine themselves.

Of the sacrament of the Lord's Supper

Q. What does the Lord's Supper signify to us?
A. That our souls are fed with the body and blood of Christ.

Q. Why is this represented by bread and wine?
A. Because what the one does to the body the same does the other to the soul spiritually.

Q. But our bodies are joined corporally with the elements or outward signs?
A. Even so are our souls joined spiritually with Christ his body.

Q. What need is there of this union with him?
A. Otherwise we cannot enioy his benefits.

Q. Declare that in the sacrament?
A. As we see the elements given to feed our bodies. Even so we see by faith Christ gave his body to us to feed our souls.

Q. Did he not give it upon the cross for us?
A. Yes, and here he gives the same body to be our spiritual food which we receive and feed on by faith.

Q. When is his body and blood our food?
A. When we feel the efficacy and power of his death in our consciences.

Q. By what way is this done?
A. By his offering and our receiving of it.

Q. How does he offer his body and blood?
A. By the word of sacraments.

Q. How do we receive his body and blood?
A. Only by our own lively faith.

Q. What follows upon this receiving by faith?
A. That Christ dwells in us and we in him.

Q. Is not this done by the Word and baptism?
A. Yes, but our joining with Christ is more evident and manifest here.

Q. Why is it more evident?
A. Because it is expressed by meat and drink joined with us inwardly in our bodies.

The parts of the sacrament and their signification

Q. What does this bread and wine signify to us?
A. Christ's body and blood once offered upon the cross for us and now given to us to be the food of our souls.

Q.What signifies that breaking of that bread?
A. The breaking and suffering of Christ's body upon the cross.

Q. What does the pouring out of the wine mean?
A.The shedding of his blood, even to the death.

Q. Where does the Supper lead us?
A. Directly to the cross and death of Christ.

Q. Should we offer him again for our sins?
A. No, for Christ did that once for all upon the cross.

Q. What things are we commanded here?
A. To take it, eat it, and drink it in his remembrance.

Q. What does the giving of that bread and wine mean?
A. The giving of Christ's body and blood to our souls.

Q. Is it not first given to our bodies?
A. No, for it is the only food of our souls.

Q. What signifies the taking of that bread and wine?
A. The spiritual receiving of Christ's body in our souls.

Q. What does our corporal eating and drinking here mean?
A. Our spiritual feeding upon the body and blood of Christ.

Q. By what way is this done?
A. By the continual exercise of our faith in Christ.

Q. What does the close conjunction we have with meat and drink mean?
A. That spirituall union which we have with Jesus Christ.

Q. What signifies the comfort we receive of meat and drink?
A. The spiritual fruits which we receive of Christ.

Q. Why is both meat and drink given here?
A. To testify that only Christ is the whole food of our souls.

Q. Does the cup appertaine to the common people?
A. Yes and the wisdom of God did so to teach us and command.

Q. Is Christ's body and blood in that bread and wine?
A. No, his body and blood is only in heaven.

Q. Why then are the elements called his body and blood?
A. Because they are sure seals of his body and blood given to us.

Christ's natural body is received

Q. Then we receive only the tokens and not his body?
A. We receive his very substantial body and blood by faith.

Q. How can that be proven?
A. By the truth of his Word and nature of a sacrament.

Q. But his natural body is in heaven?
A. Without a doubt, but yet we receive it in earth by faith.

Q. How can that be?
A. By the wonderful working of the Holy Spirit.

Q. What should we behold in this sacrament?
A. The visible food for our bodies and the inward food of our souls.

Q. Should we seek the food of our souls in the elements of bread and wine?
A. No, for they were not given to that end.

Q. To what end then were they given?
A. To lead us directly to Christ who only is the food of our souls.

Q. What profit should our bodies have by this sacrament?
A. It is a pledge of our resurrection by Christ.

Q. Why is that?
A. Because our bodies are partakers of the sign of life.

The order and use of this sacrament

Q. How should this sacrament be administered and used?
A. As Christ with his apostles did practice and command.

Q. May the minister alone use it in the name of the rest?
A. No, for it is a common and public banquet.

Q. What makes this action holy?
A. Christ's ordinance practiced by the lawful minister.

Q. How is it made fruitful?
A. Through the true faith of the receivers.

Q. To whom should this sacrament be given?
A. To all that believe and can examine themselves.

How we should prepare ourselves?

Q. What should they examine?
A. If they be lively members of Christ.

Q. How may they know this secret?
A. By their own faith and repentance.

Q. How may faith and repentance be known?
A. By their fruits agreeable to the first and second table.

Q. But all men's faith and repentance is imperfect?
A. Therefore we come to the sacrament for remedy.

Q. What kind of faith and repentance is required?
A. That which is true, upright, and not counterfeited.

Q. What do they receive comes with guilty conscience?
A. They eat and drink their own damnation.

Q. How can Christ received bring damnation?
A. He is not received by the wicked, but refused, and that by dissimulation and abuse of the sacrament.

Q. Then it is best to abstain from the sacrament?
A. We are not so commanded, but to examine and prepare ourselves.

Q. What if men cannot examine themselves?
A. Then they should read the Scriptures and consult with their pastors.

Q. What if men will not use these means?
A. Then they deceive themselves and abuse the sacrament.

Q. What if the minister admits such careles men?
A. He does then profane this holy sacrament

Of the ministry of men and the discipline

Q. How should men be excluded from the sacrament?
A. By the judgment of the elders of the church.

Q. What kind of men should be excluded?
A. All unbelievers and public slanderers of the church.

Q. What if their crime is secret?
A. Then they should be left to their own judge.

Q. Why are men excluded from the sacraments?
A. Least they should hurt themselves, slander the church, and dishonor God.

Q. By whom and when should such persons be admitted?
A. By the eldership after just trial of their repentance.

Q. Who established this order in the church?
A. Jesus Christ by his word and the apostles.

Q. What is the office of this eldership?
A. They should watch over the manners of men and exercise the discipline.

Q. What authority do they have?
A. Authority to bind and loose on earth.

Q. Can they do this at their own pleasure?
A. No, for their authority is bound to the Word.

Q. What, then, is the service of the civil magistrate?
A. He should cause all things to be done according to God's Word and defend the discipline.

Q. Does the care of the religion appertain to him?
A. No doubt seeing he is raised chiefly for this cause.

Q. Can the magistrate use the office of the ministers?
A. No, but he charges them to use their own office.

Q. What can the eldership do to the magistrate?
A. Admit him to the sacraments or exclude according to the Word of God.

Q. Can the minister use the office of the magistrate?
A. No, for they should not be entangled with worldly affairs.

Two jurisdictions in the Church

Q. How many jurisdictions are there in the church?
A. Two, one spiritual and the other civil.

Q. How do they agree in the church?
A. As the mouth and hand of God.

Q. To what end were they established in the church.
A. For the planting and preservation of the same.

Q. How far should we obey these jurisdictions?
A. So far as their commandment agrees with the Word.

Q. What should we do when they are both against the church?
A. We should remain with the church of God.

Q. But they will say the church ought to be with them?
A. We should try their sayings by the tokens of the true church.

Q. What are these signs or marks?
A. The Word, the sacraments, and discipline rightly used.

Q. What if no order of discipline exists among them?
A. Then we should remain with the Word and sacraments.

Q. But what if both the Word and sacraments be corrupted?
A. Then we should not join ourselves with that company.

Q. But what if they receive the name of the true church?
A. Satan too clothed himself with the angel of light for the further blinding of the world.

Q. But what shall men do when they do not know another church?
A. Let them content themselves with true faith in Christ.

Q. But then they are divided from the church?
A. Not from the true church and body of Christ.

Q. How can that be proven?
A. Thus: all that are united with Christ are joined with the church.

Q. Which of these two unions is first and cause of the other?
A. Our mystical and spiritual union with Jesus Christ. For we are joined with all the saints of God because we are first joined with God in Christ.

Q. What comfort, then, is our society with the church to us?
A. A singular comfort, chiefly when we are persecuted by the bastard church and tyrants of the world.

Q. How does this comfort us?
A. This, that they cannot separate us from Christ and his members albeit they separate us from their wicked society.

9.
THE FIRST CAUSE OF OUR SALVATION IS GOD'S ETERNAL ELECTION AND HERE THE PROGRESS OF THE SAME AND THE TWO ENDS OF ALL FLESH ARE DECLARED

Q. Out of what fountain does our stability flow?
A. Out of God's eternal and unchanging election in Christ.

Q. How does this election come to us?
A. By his effectual calling in due time.

Q. What works this effectual calling in us?
A. The obedience of faith.

Q. What does faith work?
A. Our perpetual and inseparable union with Christ.

Q. What works this union with Christ?
A. A mutual communion with him and his graces.

Q. What works this communion?
A. Remission of sins and imputation of justice.

Q. What works remission of sins and imputation of justice?
A. Peace of conscience and continual sanctification.

Q. What works sanctification?
A. The hatred of sin and love of godliness.

Q. What works the hatred of sin?
A. A continual battle against sin.

Q. What works this battle?
A. Continual desire to profit in godliness.

Q. What works this desire?
A. An earnest study in the Word of God.

Q. What works this earnest study?
A. A further knowledge of our own weakeness and God's goodness.

Q. What works this knowledge in us?
A. An earnest calling upon God for help.

Q. What works this earnest calling?
A. Victory against Satan and sin.

Q. What works this victory?
A. A lively experience of God's favor.

Q. What works this lively experience?
A. Boldness to fight and sure hope of further victory.

Q. What works this sure hope?
A. An unspeakeable joy of heart in trouble.

Q. What works this joy of heart?
A. Patience to the end of the battle.

Q. What works patience in us?
A. Stoutness of heart to the final triumph.

Q. What works this stoutness of heart?
A. A plain defiance against Satan and sin.

Q. What is this defiance?
A. The beginning of the eternal life in us.

Q. What is this beginning to us?
A. A sure seal of our election and glorification.

The certainty of adoption

Q. Can this seal not be abolished through sin?
A. No, for these giftes are without repentance.

Q. But many fall shamefully from God.
A. The spirit of adoption raises all the chosen again.

Q. But many are never raised again?
A. These were never the chosen of God.

Q. Yet both they and the church believed otherwise?
A. They deceived themselves but the church judges charitably.

Q. Then faith is not certain?
A. True faith is ever certain to the believers.
Q. What certainty has every one of his faith?
A. The testimony of the Spirit of adoption with the fruits.

Q. But many glory in this testimony in vain?
A. Yet this testimony is most sure and certain.

Q. Why then are so many deceived by this way?
A. Because they glory in a faith without fruits.
Q. How can we eschew this danger?
A. By the right trial of our adoption.

The trial of our adoption

Q. Where should we begin our trial?
A. At the fruits of faith and repentance because they are best known to ourselves and others.

Q. What if we begin at election?
A. Then we shall wander in darkeness.

Q. But God's election is most clear and certain?
A. It is clear and certain in itself, but it is not always certain to us in special.

Q. When is it certain to every one of us?
A. When it may be felt and known by the fruits.

Q. But this exact trial has brought some to desperation?
A. Yet God's elect are always sustained and finally comforted.

Q. Yet this trial is troublesome to men's consciences?
A. But at length it brings great peace of conscience.

Q. When and how is that?
A. When after the seeling of God's judgments we taste of his mercy again more abundantly.

Q. Why are God's elect so often thus troubled in mind?
A. That they may the better feel and know the mercy of God.

Q. Why do worldly men esteem so little the mercy of God?
A. Because they do not thoroughly taste of his justice.

Q. What, then, is trouble with the comfort of the Spirit?
A. A seal of God's love and a preparation to eternal life.

Q. What is prosperity without the taste of the Spirit?
A. A token of God's wrath and a way to perdition.

Q. But some are troubled in mind without any relief?
A. Such men begin their hell with Cain.

Of the last and eternal estate of mankind

Q. What then shall be the final end of all flesh?
A. Either life or death eternal without any change.

Q. With whom and where shall the faithful be?
A. With God in heaven full of all joy and blessedness.

Q. With whom and where shall the wicked be?
A. With Satan in hell oppressed with infinite miseries.

Q. Are these two ends certain and sure?
A. Yes no doubt, since the means are certain and sure.

Q. What are these sure means?
A. Faith and infidelity with their fruits.

Q. What makes these means sure?
A. God's most just and constant will revealed in his Word.

Q. When did he ordain these means and ends?
A. Before all beginnings in his secret counsel.
Q. To what end did he do this?
A. That his mercy and justice might shine perfectly in mankind.

Q. How was this brought to pass?
A. Through the creation of man in uprightness and his fall from that estate.

Q. What followed upon this fall of man?
A. All men once were concluded under sin and most just condemnation.

Q. How did this serve his mercy and justice?
A. Occassion was thus offered both of mercy and justice.

Q. To whom was mercy promised and given?
A. Only to his chosen children in Christ which are called the vessels of mercy.

Q. How does he show mercy to them?
A. He gives them the means whereby they come assuredly to eternal life.

Q. On whom does he show justice?
A. On all the rest of Adam's posterity which are called the children of wrath.

Q. When does he do this?
A. When he suffers them patiently to walk according to their own corrupt nature.

Q. What follows upon that walking?
A. Eternal perdition infallibly according to God's eternal decree.

Q. Does God compel them to walk that way?
A. No, but they do willingly embrace it against his word.

Q. How can men willingly eimbrace the way of perdition?
A. Because they are blinded and corrupted by Satan and their own lusts.

Q. Can they embrace the way of life?
A. No, they refuse it necessarily and yet freely without any compulsion.

Q. Where does this necessity come from?
A. From the bondage of sin in which they were cast by the fall of Adam.

Q. Is all Adam's posterity equally in the same bondage?
A. Yes no doubt but yet the chosen are redeemed through Christ and the others justly left in their natural estate.

Q. What shall be seen perpetually in the vessels of wrath?
A. The glory of God's eternal and fearful justice.

Q. What shall be seen in the vessels of mercy?
A. The perpetual praise of his mercy and goodness through Jesus Christ our Lord. To whom with the Father and the Holy Spirit be all honor and glory eternally. Amen.

10.
A SHORT AND GENERAL CONFESSION OF THE TRUE CHRISTIAN FAITH AND RELIGION, ACCORDING TO GOD'S WORD, SUBSCRIBED BY THE KING'S MAJESTY, AND HIS HOUSEHOLD, ETC.

At Edinburgh the 20th of June, 1580 and in the 14th Year of his reign.

We all, and every one of us underwritten, protest that after long and due examination of our own consciences in matters of true and false religion are now thoroughly resolved in the truth by the Word and Spirit of God. And therefore we believe with our hearts, confess with our mouths, and subscribe with our hands, and constantly affirm before God and the whole world that this is only the true Christian faith and religion pleasing God and bringing salvation to man which is now by the mercy of God revealed to the world by the preaching of the blessed gospel and is received, believed, and defended by many and various notable churches and realms, but chiefly by the church of Scotland, the king's majesty, and three estates of this realm as God's eternal truth and only ground of our salvation as more particularly is expressed in the confession of our faith established and publicly confirmed by various Acts of Parliament and now of a long time has been openly professed by the king's majesty and whole body of the realm both in city and country.

To which confession and form of religion we willingly agree in our consciences in all points as unto God's undoubted truth and verity grounded only upon his written word. And therefore we abhore and detest all contrary religion and doctrine, but chiefly all kinds of Papistry in general and particular even as they are now damned and confuted by the Word of God and church of Scotland.

But in special we detest and refuse the usurped authority of the Roman Antichrist over the Scriptures of God, over the church, the civil magistrates, and consciences of men – all this tryannous laws made upon indifferent things against our Christian liberty, his erronious doctrine against the sufficency of the written Word and perfection of the law, the office of Christ, and his blessed gospel, his corrupted doctrine concerning original sin, our natural inhability, and rebellion to God's law, his blasphemy against our justification by faith only, our imperfect satisfaction, and obedience to the law and the nature, number, and use of the holy sacraments. We detest his five bastard sacraments with all his rites, ceremonies, and false doctrine, added to the administration of the true sacraments, without the Word of God: his cruel judgments against infants departing without the sacrament, his absolute necessity of baptism, his blasphemous opinion of transubstantiation, or real prefence of Christ's body in the sacrament, and receiving of the same by the wicked, or body's of men, his dipensations with solemn oaths, perjuries, and degrees of marriage forbidden in the Word, and his cruelty against the innocent divorced.

We abhore his devilish mass, his blasphemous priesthood, his profane sacrifice for the sins of the dead and the quick, his canonization of men and women saints, calling upon angels or saints departed, worshipping of imagery, relics, crosses, dedicating of churches, altars, days, vows to creatures, his purgatory, prayer for the dead, praying or speaking in a strange language, his processions and blasphemous Letany, his multittude of advocates, or mediators, with his manifold orders, and auricular confession, his desperate and uncertain repentance, his general and doubting faith, his satisfactions of men for their sins, his justification by works, his *opus operatum*, works of supererogation, merits, pardons, peregrinations, and stations.

We detest his profane holy water, baptizing of bells, conjuring of spirits, crossing, signing, anointing, conjuring, his hallowing of God's good creatures, with the superstitious opinion joined therewith, his worldly monarchy, and wicked hierarhy, his three solemned vows, with all his shavelings of a variety of sorts; his erroneous and bloody decrees made at Trent, with all the subscribers and approvers of that cruel and bloody band, conjured against the church of God. And finally we detest all his vain allegories, rites, signs, and traditions brought in the church; without or against the Word of God and doctrine of this reformed church.

To which we join ourselves willingly in doctrine, faith, religion, discipline, and use of the holy sacraments, as lively members of the same with Christ our head, promising and swearing by the great name of our Lord, that we shall continue in the obedience of the doctrine and discipline of this church, and shall defend the same, acccording to our vocation, and power, all the days of our lives, under the pains contained in the law, and danger both of body and soul, in the day of God's fearful judgment.

And seeing that many are stirred up by Satan and the Roman antichrist to promise, swear, subscribe, and for a time use the holy sacraments in the church deceitfully against their own consciences, minding hereby first, under the external cloak of religion, to corrupt and subvert secretly God's true religion within the church, and afterward, when time may serve, to become open enemies and persecutors of the same, under vain hope of the Pope's dispensation, devised against the Word of God, to his greater confusion, and their double condemnation in the day of the Lord Jesus. We, therefore, willing to take away all suspicion of hypocrisy and of such double dealing with God and his church, protest, and call the searcher of all hearts for witness that our minds and hearts do fully agree with this our confession, promise, oath, and subscription, so that we are not moved for any worldly respect, but are persuaded only in our consciences through the knowledge and love of God's true religion imprinted in our hearts by the Holy Spirit as we shall answer to him in the day when the secrets of all hearts shall be disclosed.

And because we perceive that the quietness and stability of our religion and church does depend upon the safety and good behavior of the king's majesty as upon a comfortable instrument of God's mercy granted to this country for the maintaining of his church and ministration of justice among us, we protest and promise with our hearts that we shall defend his person and authority with our bodies and lives in the defence of Christ's gospel, liberty of our country, administration of justice, and punishment of iniquity against all enemies within this realm or without as we desire our God to be a strong and merciful defender to us in the day of our death and coming of our Lord Jesus Christ. To whom with the Father and the Holy Spirit be all honor and glory eternally, Amen.

The names of all the subscribers contained in the principal copy, written in parchment, and kept in the hands of the ministers.

The King's Majesty's charge to all the commissioners and Ministers within this Realm.

Seeing that we and our houshold have subscribed and given this public confession of our faith to the good example of our subjects, we command and charge all commissioners and ministers to require the same confession of their parishioners and to proceed against the refusers, according to our laws and order of the church, delivering their names and lawful process to the ministers of our house with all haste and diligence under the pain of 40 pounds to be taken from their stipends, that we with the advice of our counsel may take order with such proud contemners of God and our laws: subscribed with our hand. At Holyroodhouse, the 11th day of March 1580, the 14th year of our reign.

ANE

FORM

OF

EXAMINATION

BEFORE THE

COMMUNION,

APPROVED BY THE

GENERAL ASSEMBLY OF THE KIRK

OF SCOTLAND:

And appointed to be used in

FAMILIES and SCHOOLES

WITH THE

Short *Latin* Catechism,

Commonly taught in Schools

EDINBURGH,

Printed by JAMES WATSON, His Majesty's printer

MDCCXXI.

A FORM OF EXAMINATION BEFORE COMMUNION, APPROVED BY THE GENERAL ASSEMBLY OF THE KIRK OF SCOTLAND AND APPOINTED TO BE USED IN FAMILIES AND SCHOOLES (1590)

BY

JOHN CRAIG

The following is John Craig's shorter catechism commonly referred to as *Communion Catechism* in its entirety originally published in 1590. The English has been modernized.

CONTENTS

A FORM OF EXAMINATION BEFORE COMMUNION

I. Of our miserable Bondage through Adam

Q1. What are we by nature?
A. The children of God's wrath.

Ephesians 2:3

Q2. Were we thus created of God?
A. No, for he made us to his own image.

Genesis 1:26

Q3. How did we come to this misery?
A. Through the Fall of Adam from God.

Genesis 3

Q4. What things came to us by that Fall?
A. Original sin and natural corruption.

Romans 5:12, 18, 19

Q5. What power do we have to turn to God?
A. None at all, for we are dead in sin.

Ephesians 2:1

Q6. What is the punishment of our sin?
A. Death eternal, in both body and soul.

Romans 6:23

II. Of our Redemption by Christ

Q7. Who can deliver us from this bondage?
A. Only God can bring life out of death.

Q8. How do we know he will do it?
A. By his promise and by sending his Son Christ Jesus in our flesh.

John 3:16-17

Q9. What kind of person is Christ?
A. Perfect God and perfect Man without Sin.

Matthew 1:23; Luke 1:31

Q10. What was the need of this wonderful union?
A. That he might be a suitable Mediator for us.

Q11. How did he redeem us?
A. Through his obedience to the Law and death on the cross.

Philippians 2:8

Q12. Did he only suffer a natural death?
A. No, but also suffered the curse of God in both body and soul.

Galatian 3:13

Q13. How do we know his death brought life to us?
A. By his glorious resurrection and ascension

Q14. How is that?
A. For if he has not satisfied all our sins perfectly, he has not risen, nor we by him.

1 Corinthians 15:14, 17

Q15. Must we believe these mysteries?
A. No doubt, but that is not enough.

James 2:17, 20

Q16. What more is required?

A. That we be made partakers of Christ and his merits.
John 15.4-7

III. Of our Participation with Christ

Q17. How is that produced?
A. Through his continual intercession for us in heaven.
Hebrews 7:25

Q18. Explain how that is done.
A. Hereby the Holy Spirit is sent.
John 14:16, 26

Q19. What does the Spirit do in this work?
A. He offers Christ and his graces to us and moves us to receive him.

Q20. How does he offer Christ to us?
A. By the preaching of the evangel.
Romans 10:13-15

Q21. How does he move us to receive him?
A. Through printing in our hearts true faith in Christ.
Acts 16:14

Q22. What is faith in Christ?
A. A sure persuasion that he is the only Savior of the world, but ours in special who beleive in him.
John 6

Q23. What does this fruit work?
A. Our inseparable union with Christ and his graces.
Ephesians 3:16-19

Q24. What is the first fruit of this union?

A. A remission of our sins and imputation of righteousness.

Romans 6:19

Q25. What is the second fruit of our union with him?
A. Our sanctification and regeneration to the image of God.

John 3:3-5

Q26. Who does this and how?
A. The Holy Spirit through our union with Christ in his death, burial, and resurrection.

Romans 6

Q27. What are the chief parts of our regeneration?
A. Mortification of sin and rising to righteousness.

Romans 6

Q28. How do we know sin and righteousness?
A. By the just and perfect Law of God.

Romans 7

IV. Of the Word

Q29. Where can we find the Word of God?
A. Only in the Holy Scriptures.

Romans 15:4

Q30. Are the Scriptures sufficient for our instruction?
A. No doubt, as the apostles do testify.

John 20:31; Galatians 1:8; 2 Timothy 3:17

Q31. How should we receive and use the Word?
A. We should read it privately and publically with all reverence.

Deuteronomy 31:21

Q32. Is this sufficient for our instruction?
A. No, if public teaching may be had.
Ephesians 4:11-12

Q33. Why is that?
A. For as God raises public teachers and pastors so he has commanded us to hear them.
Malachi 2:7

Q34. How long should we continue in this school?
A. All the days of our lives seeing we are ignorant, forgetful, and easy to be deceived.
Colossians 3:16

Q35. What then do the sacraments serve?
A. They are added for our further comfort and admonition as a visible word.
Genesis 17:9-11; Exodus 12

V. Of our Liberty to serve God

Q36. What good things can we do now being thus regenerated?
A. We may serve our God freely and uprightly.
Romans 12

Q37. Can we do it perfectly according to the Law?
A. No truly, for our regernation is not perfect.
Galatians 5:17; Eccelsiastes 7:22

Q38. What follows from that?
A. A certain rebellion of the flesh against the Spirit.
Romans 7:15-25

Q39. Is this rebellion not cursed by the Law?
A. Yes truly, but yet it is not imputed to us.

2 Corinthians 5:19

Q40. Why is that seeing it is sin and the root of all our sins.
A. Because Christ satisfied all the points of the Law for us.

Romans 3:21ff

Q41. What are we then who believe in Christ?
A. Just in him but sinners in ourselves.

Romans 8

Q42. What does this confession require of us?
A. A constant faith in Christ and continual repentance.

Q43. What then is our only joy in life and death?
A. That all our sins past, present and future are buried and Christ only is made our wisdom, justification, sanctification, and redemption.

1 Corinthians 1:30

Q44. What fruit comes of this faith?
A. A peace of conscience and joy in the Spirit in all our troubles within and without.

Romans 5:2; 2 Corinthians 6:4

Q45. What shall we gather from this whole discourse?
A. How miserable we are through Adam and how blessed we are through Christ.

Philippians 3:8

Q46. When should we remember from this doctrine?
A. At all times, but chiefly when we are touched with a proud opinion of our own worthiness or are troubled in conscience of sin.

Luke 18:19

Q47. Then this meditation serves for a preparation to the holy sacraments?
A. Yes, truly if they be rightly considered.

VI. Of the Sacraments

Q48. Explain that in baptism.
A. We see there the seal of our spiritual filthiness through our communion with Adam and our purgation by our communion with Christ.

Q49. Explain the same in the supper.
A. We see, feel, and taste there also the seal of our spiritual wants and death through Adam and likewise of our spiritual treasures and life through Christ only.

Q50. How did we contract our spiritual filthiness from Adam?
A. Through our natural communion with him.

Romans 5:12ff

Q51. How did we come to our spiritual purgation and life by Christ?
A. Through our spiritual communion with our Second Adam, Head, and Spouse.

Ephesians 5:30

Q52. Do the Word and the sacraments work this communion?
A. No, for it is only the work of the Spirit.

Ephesians 3:16

Q53. Where do the Word and sacraments lead us?
A. Directly to the cross and the death of Christ.

1 Corinthians 1:17-18, 23-24

Q54. Why is that?
A. Because through his cross and death the wrath of God was quenched and all his blessings made ours.

Galatians 3:13-14

Q55. Why was this high mystery represented by these weak and common elements?
A. Because they express most lively our spiritual purging and feeding which we have by Christ.

John 6:32ff

Q56. When does he do these things?
A. When he is so joined with us and we with him that he abides in us and we in him spiritually.

John 15:4-5

Q57. How is this union and abiding expressed here?
A. By natural washing, eating, drinking, digesting, feeding, and abiding in us.

Q58. How may we feel and know this spiritual abiding in us?
A. By the testimony of the Spirit in us and external actions agreeable to Christ in us.

Matthew 7:6; Romans 8:16

Q59. Then Christ is not an idle guest in us?
A. No truly, for he came not only with water and blood, but also with the Spirit to assure us in some measure of his presence in us.

1 John 5:6

VII. Of Baptism

Q60. What does baptism signify?
A. That we are filthy by nature and are purged by the blood of Christ.

Titus 3:5

Q61. What does our union with the water mean?
A. Our spiritual union with Jesus Christ.

Romans 6:3, 8; Galatians 3:27

Q62. What follows upon our union with him?
A. Remission of sins and regeneration.

Romans 6:4, 18, 22

Q63. Where does our regeneration come from?
A. From the communion with the death, burial, and resurrection of Christ.

Romans 6:4-5, 8

Q64. How long and by what way does baptism work in us?
A. All the days of our life through faith and repentance.

1 Corinthians 6:19-20

Q65. How then are infants baptized?
A. Upon the promise made to the faithful and their seed.

Genesis 17:7, 10

Q66. How does baptism differ from the Supper?
A. In the elements, action, rites, signification, and use.

Q67. Why is baptism only ministered once?
A. It is enough to be received once in the house of God.
Romans 8:16

Q68. Explain the cause of that.
A. For they are never cast out who are once truly received in his society.
John 6:37

Q69. Why is the supper so often ministered?
A. We have need to be fed continually.
John 6:35

Q70. Why is the supper not ministered to infants?
A. Because they cannot examine themselves.
1 Corinthians 11:18

VIII. Of the Supper

Q71. What does the action of the supper signify?
A. That our souls are fed spiritually by the body and blood of Jesus Christ.
John 6:54

Q72. When is this done?
A. When we feel the efficacy of his death in our conscience by the Spirit of faith.
John 6:63

Q73. Why is this sacrament given in meat and drink?
A. To seal up our near conjunction with Christ.

Q74. Why are both meat and drink given?
A. To testify that Christ is the whole food of our souls.

John 6

Q75. Is Christ's body in the elements?
A. No, but it is in heaven.

Acts 1:11

Q76. Why, then, is the element called his body?
A. Because it is a sure seal of his body given to our souls.

Q77. To whom should this sacrament be given?
A. Only to the faithful who can examine themselves.

Q78. In what ways should they examine themselves?
A. In faith and repentance with their fruits.

Q79. What should the pastors do when men are negligent and abuse the sacraments?
A. They should use the order of discipline established in the Word.

IX. Of Discipline

Q80. Who should use this discipline?
A. The pastors and elders by their mutual consent and judgment.

Q81. What is the offie of the eldership?
A. To watch upon their flock and exercise the discipline.

Q82. How is this done?
A. By private and public admonition and other censures of the Kirk as need requires.

Q83. Who ought to be excluded from the sacraments?
A. All infidels and public slanderers.

Q84. Why are these excluded?
A. Lest they should hurt themselves, slander the Kirk, and dishonor God.

X. Of the Magistrate

Q85. What is the office of the Christian Magistrate in the Kirk?
A. He should defend the true religion and discipline and punish all troublers and dispisers.

XI. Of the Table in Special

Q86. Why do we use a table here and not an altar as the Fathers did at God's commandment?
A. Because we convene not to offer a sacrifice for sin, but to eat and drink of that sacrifice which Christ once offered upon the cross for us.

Hebrews 7:23-24, 27, 10:11-12, 14, 18

Q87. What do we profess when we come to the table?
A. That we are dead in ourselves and seek only our life in Christ.

Q88. Shall this confession of our unworthiness be a stay to come to the communion?
A. No truly, but rather a preparation to the same if faith and repentance be with it.

Mark 2:17

Q89. Why is there mention made here of Christ' body and

blood in particular?
A. To testify his death by which only he was made our spiritual meat and drink.

John 6:51, 55

Q90. For what cause is this action called the communion?
A. Because it is the true cause of our mutual society with Christ in all things, good and evil.

Q91. Explain how that is performed.
A. He removes all evil things from us which we have by nature and we receive of him all good things which we want by nature.

Q92. Explain these things more plainly.
A. The wrath of God and sin is removed which we have by nature and the favor of God and adoption with the joy of heaven is restored to us the things which we do not have by nature.

Romans 8

Q93. What then may the faithful soul say?
A. Now I live, yet not I, but Christ lives in me. It is God that justifies who shall condemn.

Q94. Let us therefore give thanks and pass to this holy action every one of us saying and singing in his heart, the Lord is the portion of mine inheritance and of my cup, you shall maintain my lot, the lines are fallen unto me in pleasant places, yes, I have a fair heritage. Psalm 15:5-6
A. Let it be done so with heart and mouth to the confusion of all idolaters and glory of our God.

XII. The End of our Redemption.

Q95. To what end are we thus redeemed and brought in hope of that endless joy to come?
A. To move us effectually to deny all ungodliness, worldly lusts, and unrighteousness, and so live godly, soberly, and righteoussly in this present world, looking for the coming of Christ, for our full redemption.

Titus 2:11-13

Q96. What shall be the final end of all these graces?
A. God shall be glorified forever in mercy and we shall enjoy that endless life with Christ our Head to whom, with the Father and the Holy Spirit, be all honor and glory forever. Amen.

FINIS

BORN 1512 DIED 1600

RECOMMENDED READING

Below is a short list of helpful books on John Craig's life, ministry, influence, work, and theology. Because John Knox is the most recognizable and influential figure in the Scottish Reformation of the 16th Century, Craig is mentioned and highlighted as his collegue and fellow Reformer. Thus, some of the best resources on Craig are biographies and books on Knox. John Knox's *History of the Reformation in Scotland* provides some of the most relevant and early history of Craig.

Books

Beenedetto, Robert. *The New Westminister Dictionary of Church History, Volume One: The Early, Medieval, and Reformation Eras*. Louisville, Westminister John Knox Press, 2008.

Bonar, Horatius. *Catechisms of the Scottish Reformation*. London: James Nisbet & Co., 1866.

Church of Scotland. *A Collection of Confessions of Faith,*

Catechisms, Directories, Books of Discipline, &c. Volume 2. Edinburgh, 1722.

Cochrane, Arthur C, ed. *Reformd Confessions of the Sixteenth Century*. Louisville: Westminister John Knox, 2003.

Craig, John. *A Shorte Summe of the Whole Catechisme*. Edited by Thomas Graves Law. Edinburgh: David Douglas, 1883.

Dennison, James T. *Reformd Confessions of the 16th and 17th Centuries in English Translation.* 4 vols. Reformation Heritage Books, 2008-2014.

Foggie, Janet P. *Renaissance Religion in Urban Scotland: The Dominican Order, 1450-1560.* Brill Academic Pub, 2003.

Howie, John. *The Scot Worthies*. New York: Robert Carter and Brothers, 1853.

Irving, Edward. *The Confessions of Faith and the Book of Discipline of the Church of Scotland, of Date Anterior to the Westminister Confession.* London: Paternoster-Row, 1831.

Johnston, John C. *Treasurey of the Scottish Covenant.* Edinburgh, 1887.

Kerr, T. A. *John Craig (1512? - 1600) : with special reference to his contribution to the upbuilding of the Reformd Church in Scotland.* Edinburgh: University of Ediburgh, 1954.

Knox, John. *The Works of John Knox, Volumes 1 and 2: History of the Reformation in Scotland.* Eugene, OR: Wipf & Stock, 2004.

Lang, Andrew. *John Knox and the Reformation*. New York: Longmans, Green, and Co., 1905.

Law, Thomas Graves. *Collected Essays and Reviews of Thomas graves law, LL.D.* Edited by P. Hume Brown. Ediburgh: T & A Constable; 1904.

MackIntosh, John. The *History of Civilisation in Scotland.* Volume 2. London: Alexander Gardner, 1893.

M'Crie, Thomas. *The Life of Andrew Melville: Containing Illustrtations of the Ecclesiastical and Literary History of Scotland, duirng hte latter part of the Sixteenth and Beginning of the Seventeenth Century*. Edinburgh: 1819.

________. *The Life of John Knox: Containing Illustrations of the History of the Rformation in Scotland; with Biographical Notices of the Principal Reformsr, and Sketches of the Progress of Literature in Scotland, During a great Part of the Sixteenth Century*. Edinburgh: 1814.

Memorials of the Dawn of the Reformation in Europe. London: Thomas Nelson, 1847.

Schaff, Philip. *The Creeds of Christendom*. 3 vols. Grand Rapids: Baker, 1876.

Presbyterian Church in the U.S.A. Board of Publication. *The Bishop and the Monk, or, Sketches of the Lives of Pierpaolo Vergerio and John Craig, Converts from Popery*. Philadelphia: Presbyterian Board of Publication, 1857.

Row, John. *History of the Kird of Scotland 1558-1637*. Edinburgh: Woodrow Society, 1842.

Story, Robert Herbert. *Dr. John Craig, 1512-1600: A Lecture Delivered in the West Kirk, Edinburgh on the evening of Sunday the 10th February 1884*. Edinburgh, 1884.

Torrance, Thomas F. *Scottish Theology: From John Knox to John McLeod Campbell.* T&T Clark, 2001.

________. *The School of Faith: The Catechisms of the Reformd Church.* Eugene, OR: Wipf & Stock Publishers, 1996.

Trueman, Carl R. *The Creedal Imperative.* Wheaton, IL: Crossway, 2012.

Tytler, Patrick Fraser. *The Life of Sir Thomas Craig of Riccarton with Biographical Scetches of His Most Eminent Legal Contemporaries.* Edinburgh, Printed for W & C. Tait, 1823.

Walker, Alexander. *John Craig 1512-1600: An Aberdeenshire Scot, a friar of the order of S. Dominic, Rector of the University of Bologna, preacher of the New Evangel in Edinburgh, - in Montrose, in Aberdeen, and one of the ministers to His Majesty's Grace James Sext.* Aberdeen, 1889.

Internet

"John Craig." *Oxford Dictionary of National Biography.* http://www.oxforddnb.com/view/article/6574; Internet.

ABOUT THE EDITOR

Kyle McDanell is the pastor at Goshen Baptist Church in Falls of Rough, Kentucky. He has an undergraduate degree in Biblical and Theological Studies from Boyce College and both an Advanced Masters of Divinity and a Master of Theology (Th.M) in Systematic Theology from the Southern Baptist Theological Seminary in Louisville, KY. He is the author of *Logizomai: A Reasonable Faith in an Unreasonable World* (Resource Publishings, 2012) and *The Death of Death: Confronting the Culture of Death With the Gospel of Christ* (Createspace, 2013). Kyle has been married since July 2006 to his high school swetheart and has two children.

Check out his blog at www.kylemcdanell.com.

OTHER TITLES BY KYLE MCDANELL

How should Christians think and engage the culture of death we now live in? Every day new challenges regarding abortion, euthanasia, infanticide, eugenics, and biotechnology force Christians to consider the conclusions of Christian theology and how to minister to those who are hurting. Typically, Christians articulate what they are against, but rarely show how the gospel offers a better way. This book seeks not only to help the average believer understand the many challenges of the culture of death, but also to show how the gospel informs our Christian worldview and how it offers hope even in a culture of blood like ours. Being a pro-life Christian means more than just voting for pro-life candidates and supporting pro-life causes. A pro-life Christian must also show the world the power of the gospel, the love of the Father, the peace of Christ, and the beauty of the local church. Christians must not just condemn the culture, but offer the grace of Christ that touches the lives of those in the culture. It is a call to understand the challenges of the culture of death and, at the same time, a call for Christians to actively seek the end of this culture that is consumed with blood.

OTHER TITLES BY KYLE MCDANELL

"We live in a world of information overload. The internet has given rise to millions of voices clamoring for attention, leading to massive confusion regarding the truth. Kyle McDanell is a thoughtful blogger who speaks forcefully and clearly in this world of internet noise. Over and over again, he goes right to the heart of the matter, illuminating current issues through the lens of biblical truth."

—TREVIN WAX, author of *Holy Subversion: Allegiance to Christ in an Age of Rivals* and *Counterfeit Gospels: Rediscovering the Good News in a World of False Hope*

Made in the USA
Coppell, TX
02 May 2022

77328764R00129